Eurythmics, 1983

1980s NEWCASTLE

Memories from people who were there

Edited by Anna Flowers and Vanessa Histon

Tyne Bridge Publishing

Tyne Bridge Publishing and Newcastle Libraries sincerely thank all our contributors, who gave so generously of their time, memories, photographs, and memorabilia. This book is by you, and for you. We were not able to include everything that was sent to us, and we apologise to those whose memories we could not fit in. We hope that the following pages give an authentic flavour of some of the things that mattered to the people of Newcastle in the 1980s. If it isn't here, then you didn't tell us about it!

Thanks to Mirrorpix, Rex Features, TTTV, and countless others for their help with sourcing illustrations.

Unless otherwise indicated illustrations are from the collections of, or are copyright of, Newcastle Libraries.

Front cover: Polly Rutter models a Newby Priory dress, Handyside Arcade, 1987 ©Elspeth Rutter

Cover design by StadtCreative.com

The views expressed in this book are solely those of the contributors and in no way reflect the views of the Council of the City of Newcastle upon Tyne.

Published by
City of Newcastle upon Tyne
Newcastle Libraries & Information Service
Tyne Bridge Publishing, 2013

www.tynebridgepublishing.co.uk
www.newcastle.gov.uk/libraries

ISBN: 978-1-85795-215-5

Printed by hpmgroup

John Coatsworth

The Bigg Market, 1980s, painted by John Coatsworth.

Right, TUC leader Len Murray (in the light coat) on Clayton Street, November 1979.

The Queen Mother goes walkabout and greets an enthusiastic crowd at Eldon Square, 16 April, 1980. It was the official start of the Newcastle 900 celebrations.

CONTENTS

A NEW ENGLAND

Kirsty McColl 1985

The 1980s began, for the UK, with a new Prime Minister, Margaret Thatcher; Leonid Brezhnev was supremo in Moscow; Ronald Reagan would soon be elected US President, and Nelson Mandela was still in prison. By the end of the decade the power of the UK unions had been crushed; city banks had been deregulated along with the buses and much else; the Berlin Wall had tumbled; Mrs Thatcher was looking at tougher times to come. Some shocking events had occurred, nationally and internationally, during the 1980s: the Falklands war; IRA bombings in London and Brighton; the agony of the Miners' Strike; urban riots; long-term unemployment; the tragedy of Chernobyl; the threat of AIDS; the horror of Lockerbie; the Heysel and Hillsborough disasters to mention just a few. It looked as though heavy industry had been irrevocably diminished at home, and the gap between rich and poor had widened everywhere.

On the other hand …

From protest marches to Greenham Common, people were actively engaged with politics, the economy seemed to be making a recovery by the mid-decade, and computers were taking off (remember Pac-man and the ZX Spectrum?). Popular culture flourished, from the energy of post-punk via the New Romantics, to the rise of House and Techno. On TV we saw the creativity of Channel 4's *The Tube*, the joy of *Spitting Image* and *The Young Ones*, the sharpness of *The Boys from the Black Stuff* and *East Enders*. There was an outpouring of compassion through Live Aid, Comic Relief, the Great North Run and much more. The soap opera of the Royal Weddings and their aftermaths kept us enthralled. Fashion went to extremes from baggy trousers to big hair and big shoulders.

What happened nationally and in the wider world was reflected in Newcastle. The change in atmosphere is evident from looking at the City Council mouthpiece, *City News*, between 1980 and 1989. At the beginning of the decade the news sheet was printed on cheap paper in black and white with red headlines and was unrelentingly gloomy in its forecasts of rate rises, cuts in services, job losses, rampant inflation, and its opposition to central government. (There were always good-news stories of course such as the celebrations surrounding Newcastle's 900th anniversary in 1980. There was always the Summer Exhibition, or visits from the RSC to look forward to and much else besides).

By the middle of the decade *City News* reported that things were looking up (though unemployment was still one in five in a population of 282,000). The rates had come down, the Tall Ships Race was coming to the city in 1986 and much regeneration was underway.

By the end of the decade, despite continuing problems of unemployment, poverty and dereliction, particularly in the west end, the Quayside was being transformed by Tyne & Wear Development Corporation, there was bustle in the shops, new bars were springing up and *City News* had embraced colour print. Content was largely dominated

Karen Laidler and boyfriend living alternatively in their flat in Fenham, mid 1980s. (Karen Laidler)

by good-news stories (though those employment figures were constantly an issue). The paper was a little less a political mouthpiece, more a feelgood information broadsheet for the Council. In 1989 it noted that the economy was looking buoyant for economic regeneration in the 1990s.

Tellingly, the last issue of the decade announced that the city had appointed the advertising agency J. Walter Thompson to help develop a marketing strategy to change perceptions of the North East. The final good-news story was the opening of the new Warner's cinema complex at Manors with the cast of *Byker Grove* and Kylie Minogue in person! The film premiered was *The Delinquents*.

Anna Flowers, Vanessa Histon

The Quayside was not a part of town where you'd want to linger in 1983. New owner Michael Quadrini wanted to site his Tuxedo Princess on the Newcastle side but the City Council would not permit it and 'The Boat' opened beneath the Tyne Bridge on the Gateshead side in September 1983.

Tuxedo Princess waits in the wings for her debut, 1983. Photographer Peter Brabban captured 'The Boat' on Newcastle Quayside. The Caledonian Princess car ferry had recently arrived from Glasgow.

Newcastle and Gateshead Quayside in 1987 as regeneration progressed. The bleak look of the early 1980s was being transformed, and Tuxedo Princess was established under the Tyne Bridge.

It's the end of the world as we know it (and I feel fine)

A description of Newcastle in 1980 might seem a little bleak to many who weren't around back then, a city devoid of almost everything they're so comfortable with today. There were no American cafés and fast-food joints, not even a McDonald's; no bright and enticing multinational chains selling designer clothes ('labels' were for washing instructions only) and nowhere to show them off in the evening anyway, with most of the pubs full of old blokes, and all closed by ten-thirty sharp.

It would be a strange and bewildering place for those who nowadays enjoy conspicuous consumption, continental-style cafés and dining, and sophisticated nightlife. Yet this was the era when all these concepts took root in Newcastle, while also being the last decade before the full blandness of modern consumerism descended on the city. Local operators dictated the way people socialised and they altered huge swathes of the cityscape to cater for them. Independent shops were always first to spot and stock the latest music and clothes when fads and fashions seemed to change completely every other year and were officially dead by the time they hit Top Shop.

One of the most significant changes to Newcastle happened early in the decade, when Joe Robertson acquired a few decrepit old pubs in the Bigg Market and transformed them into a circuit of plush and aspirational nightspots. Although the term 'yuppie' hadn't yet been coined (first usage 1984) there was an appetite for throwing money around in those early and optimistic days of Thatcher's Britain, and being seen to do so. Joe's bars and Michael Quadrini's eye-wateringly opulent Tuxedo Junction nightclub were there to catch it. In just a couple of years Newcastle's nightlife changed beyond recognition: a city of rundown pubs frequented by old gadgies and wifies was dragged out of the dark ages and was on its way to becoming an internationally renowned party destination.

Ironically, these newly fashionable bars and clubs operated strict dress codes that did nothing to encourage or embrace the sartorial excesses of the decade. You had no hope of boarding Quadrini's *Tuxedo Princess* dressed like Boy George, any member of Duran Duran or Spandau Ballet, or sporting a Katharine Hamnett-designed 'Frankie Says Relax' t-shirt. But this and other nightclubs were happy to play the music of these artistes; and indeed Frankie Goes to Hollywood, Mick Hucknall and Rick Astley were among many 80s icons for whom the rules were temporarily overlooked on their obligatory visits to 'The Boat'.

To be fair, the bouncers did the more extravagantly dressed and coiffured locals a favour, keeping them apart from the traditionally minded and easily riled Geordies on the lash. Adam Ant's famous line, 'Ridicule is nothing to be scared of', obviously wasn't written with early eighties Newcastle in mind. But this was a boom time for independent clothes shops, cashing in on all the latest 'looks'. High Bridge was lined with them, at the forefront of the emerging 'designer' culture and stocking creations by the likes of Hamnett, Betty Jackson, Jasper Conran and John Galliano. Other chancers were able to thrive alongside them – at least one shop had its suits run up for next to nowt by Westgate Road tailor Mr Rahman, whose legendary Metro Radio advert claimed he'd put a zip in anything from a topcoat to a bikini, for just one pound.

The more pioneering types made their own fashion statements, finding the raw materials in the many junk and second-hand shops around town. Or you could enter the Handyside Arcade on a Saturday afternoon and leave an hour or so later, attired and accessorised to your satisfaction from its mix of antique, punk, hippie and army surplus clothing shops in the full expectation of being barred from every mainstream pub and club in town for looking too weird. Luckily there was an alternative scene emerging, where the offbeat was embraced and individuality worshipped. A handful of local entrepreneurs hired rooms in pubs and clubs where they ran 'alternative nights', such as Mr M's at Tiffanys, The Delby above La Dolce Vita, the Gearbox at the Mayfair, and other regular events at

Balmbras, The Junction, Rockshots and Wheeler's in Gateshead.

For all the good work the likes of Joe Robertson and Michael Quadrini did in modernising Newcastle's nightlife, it was those on the 'alternative' scene who truly put Newcastle on the

Gordon Clark

Geordies on the lash. Macey's, 1988.

map. There was a circuit of bars on the periphery of the city centre that catered for those too hip, sensible or sensitive to drink in the Bigg Market. *Viz Comic* first appeared in the Gosforth Hotel, but it was pubs such as the Baltic Tavern, Trent House, Strawberry, Broken Doll, Barley Mow and Egypt Cottage that subsequently advertised in it, sold it, and were frequented by those who wrote it. And it wasn't unusual for the managers of these bars or their punters to become regular characters in *Viz*.

Looking down on the Barley Mow, 1988, from the student flats in the Keelmen's Hospital.

It was from this scene that Riverside emerged, a co-operative of music fans who drank on the circuit and wanted to create somewhere they could watch bands that had previously skipped Newcastle on their tours due to a lack of suitable venues and audiences. After an admittedly shaky start, Riverside was soon was attracting bands of national and international stature, such as Nirvana, Stone Roses and Happy Mondays. In fact, for a few years in the eighties, City Road was the coolest street outside of London on a Friday night, as crowds wandered between the marvellously relaxed and friendly Barley Mow, the nearby Riverside, and the Egypt

Cottage; the last of which would be full of people and performers who'd just appeared on *The Tube* in the Tyne Tees Television studios next door.

Let's not forget the massive impact *The Tube* had on Newcastle. It demonstrated that there was a pool of hugely innovative producers and directors outside of London who were talented and credible enough to attract some of the biggest names in the world to a far corner of England, where many of them would deliver career-defining performances. In turn, some of these employees of Tyne Tees have themselves gone on to become internationally renowned in their field. On a local level, it provided the people of Newcastle with an unprecedented and probably never to be repeated opportunity to see some of the world's biggest music legends close up – and if you were especially lucky, have a drink with them in the Egypt after the show. One evening some musicians failed to turn up at Riverside but luckily Elvis Costello happened to be at Tyne Tees, and he made the short walk along City Road to placate the angry crowd with a superb solo performance.

It was from within this 'alternative' scene, largely made up of Newcastle's bohemian set and savvy students from outside the region, that organised street-level opposition to the Conservative government and their policies began to emerge. Some had been politicised by the Falklands War in 1982, and by the time of the Miners' Strike a year or so later, their ranks had swollen considerably as thousands of people and many local bands became involved in demonstrations of support and benefit gigs for the pitmen and their families.

George Walker

Polly Rutter, Roxanne Walker and friend, ready for an alternative night out, 1985.

By the end of the decade, after some bruising encounters with the authorities over the emerging 'rave' scene, there were a considerable number of people from all backgrounds prepared to take to the streets in opposition to the Poll Tax in 1990.

The North East had been one of the powerhouses of the Industrial Revolution and the local economy was dependent on those who earned a living in the mines, shipyards, steelworks and factories. Nobody of any political persuasion could argue that the region didn't suffer terribly when its heavy industries were considered expendable. But bizarrely, the night-time economy continued to thrive. Towards the end of the decade, when Thatcher's policies took their toll on the North East workforce, the Bigg Market began its descent into an area where you went to get smashed as cheaply as possible. Many bars began selling treble measures of spirits for a quid in happy hours that seemed to last most of the evening, to a population hell-bent on having a ball while they still had some money in their pockets.

Newcastle as a whole is a notoriously late adopter of fashions and trends. There were still half a dozen 'rock bars' around the Haymarket stuck in a 1970s double denim time warp; and elsewhere punks and Goths could be chased through the Bigg Market like medieval witches. But the 'Second Summer of Love', in 1988, began the blurring of the lines between the alternative and the mainstream scenes. We were a little behind Madchester, Liverpool and London, but by the end of the decade many younger people shared a common love of rave music and the euphoric effects of its vital component, ecstasy. In fields, warehouses and peoples' homes, you started to see loved-up West End charvers hugging Home Counties art students, with everyone stinking of Vick's VapoRub and grinning like imbeciles.

You could tell the end was nigh, for this fabulously hedonistic and creative decade. For the first time in 40 years pop stars were no longer shocking or amusing the public, which was arguably their main purpose. The public didn't care anyway, because DJs were becoming the new style and musical gurus. There were still those on the margins who loved live music, but the emerging bands seemed less inspiring to the masses than the electronically generated repetitive beats and remixes of old songs; a genre that had been made easy for youths to swallow by Stock, Aitken and Waterman's domination of the charts towards the end of the eighties.

Throw in some hallucinogenic drugs and hypnotic light shows, and a new generation was primed to embrace the bleep bleep sounds and double bland fashions of the dance and rave scenes in which 'style' meant the casual sportswear look that we've been stuck with for the best part of 20 years, and opened the door in the nineties to the all-pervading abomination that is the shell suit.

The ensuing decade would see the dominance of multi-national clothing chains selling cheap and

Peter Brabban

Peter Thomson

Above, the obvious reference to Norman Tebbit's infamous quip at The People's March for Jobs, outside MEA House, in 1983.

Right, at the annual May Day march in 1988 working conditions and jobs were very much an issue as the banners head into Newcastle.

15

mass-produced uniforms for people to wear while drinking designer lagers in Newcastle bars and clubs, now owned by publicly listed corporations; or while consuming their American fast food and frothy coffees. For anyone who loved the quickly changing and often ludicrous fashion and music scenes, quirky local pubs, cafés and shops, and the unbridled celebration of individuality that was Newcastle in the 1980s, the 1990s turned out to be just a tad bleak!

Marshall Hall

Newcastle 900

In 1980 Newcastle celebrated its 900th birthday with a year-long party. Celebrations kicked off with a fireworks display in Old Eldon Square on 30 January. The Queen Mother officially inaugurated the celebrations on 16 April, dedicating a plaque in Eldon Square. On 14 June the Lord Mayor's Parade included the world's longest bucket chain of 758 metres, set up by 2,500 children. In July a powerboat

Presidents Bar, Cloth Market, 1988.

regatta was held on the Tyne and a military tattoo took place outside the Civic Centre. Other activities included a literary festival, a golf tournament, a dance festival, a marathon, and a firework fiesta on the Town Moor. On 19 December a lead-cased capsule packed with Newcastle 900 souvenirs was buried in the grounds of the Civic Centre.

The City invested in two Polyairdromes to house exhibitions (including Ideal Home, and a motor fair) by the University Theatre, but they weren't that popular, partly because of the lack of parking.

By 1982 £6,600 worth of souvenirs remained unsold, including 125 teddy bears which were sold off at the Central Library. Many of the souvenirs were given to charity. While sales made an overall profit of £31,000, Newcastle 900 cost much more than the estimated £100,000, and came under scrutiny.

Anna Flowers

Top, the souvenir shop in Eldon Square. Right, the Polyairdromes.

BAGGY TROUSERS

Madness, 1982

Oh what fun we had!

My dad was out of work in the 1980s and I had a stay-at-home mum so it was tough. Dad would say 'Things are just hunky dorey!' He was in the building trade. There were a lot of things to worry about – I was terrified about the Falklands, bombs in Beirut, nuclear war, and Chernobyl. We worried about eating lamb from Cumbria. I was a gloomy child!

Prince Charles and Lady Di got married in 1981. I was eight and was given a commemorative thimble (I still have it) as a souvenir. I have a photo of me and my brother in a Royal Wedding sweatshirt. It was the hottest day of the year and there we were in fleeces, with a picture of Charles and Di on the front. We went over to my auntie's at West Denton and they had a party in the back garden for the kids.

Lisa Webb

I went to Bolam Street Primary which was lovely. Then I went to Benfield in 1985, which was a big shock. I remember being taken to the Rainbow Rooms in the Co-op as a treat to make up for having to buy school uniform in Farnons. Benfield school was so huge. I was one of the smallest in the class and it took a while to adjust to the noise, but by the time I got to the third year I started to enjoy it. We were taken on a school trip to *Tuxedo Princess* and I remember a fantastic banner which said 'Don't walk, boogie'.

During the teachers' strikes in 1987 it was freezing cold and we would be turfed out at dinner times. It was usually snowing. I'd walk to a friend's house, eat my dinner in ten minutes and walk back to school. Kids on free school meals were given a plastic bag with a strawberry milkshake, a sandwich and some crisps. We'd flood out from school, hundreds of kids all in a rush. Later in the strike we went to school for half days. I was doing GCSEs so it was very disruptive.

I was one of just three girls in the Boys Brigade at St Michael's church hall in Byker, and we did the Duke of Edinburgh Award. There was nothing much else for girls to do in Byker.

We wore luminous orange, green and pink socks and jelly sandals.

Lisa Webb

Royal wedding celebrations on 29 July at Britannia Place, Elswick. There were street parties all over the city.

(NCJ / Mirrorpix)

Nicola Booth

Above, the school holidays and skateboards on Blackett Street, August 1988.

Left, Walker play area, 1986.

Right, teenagers Nicola Booth and friends, old Eldon Square, 1980.

1980s technology transformed the activities at Hodgkin Park. The children built their own disco equipment including lights. We got table tennis tables and pool tables but we retained a lot of the old activities such as games, sand castle making and building structures.

We travelled much further and visited a lot of other play projects. We entered a BMX rally and table tennis tournaments helped by Peter McQueen, who was number six in the world at the time.

Ken McCormick, Play Organiser at Hodgkin Park
Adventure Playground

My best and worst sporting moments came at West Jesmond Primary School. I had my one and only moment of athletic glory there aged 11, as the combative right back in the school's title-winning football team. If I'm honest, I think I largely owed my place in the team to being friends with Paul Watts, our star midfielder and coincidentally the son of our form teacher and inspirational manager. I don't like to suggest that a pillar of the community like Mr Watts might have fallen prey to nepotism but I can think of no other explanation for including a defender like me whose two main skills were badly-timed late tackles and inexplicably hoofing the ball out of play instead of passing it.

Anyway, whatever the reasons for my selection, I was delighted to be there as we made our way unchallenged through game after game, banging in more goals than any other team in the league. Coming from Jesmond, we were supposedly the 'poshies', a middle-class bunch of wimps who weren't meant to be any good at football, but, you know what, we were imperious; the Barcelona of Under 12 North-Eastern schools soccer. We even stopped one game at half time I remember because we were 8-0 up and the other team had become visibly distressed. As we clinched the title I remember scenes of epic celebration, spraying each other with fizzy apple drink. I still have the little plastic trophy I received. Not on the mantelpiece or anything, I'm not a saddo, but it's definitely in a box somewhere, along with my long-buried dreams of being a professional footballer. If only Mr Watts had got a job managing Newcastle United, I might have been in with a chance.

If that was the high point of my sporting life then the nadir had been a year or two earlier when swimming certificates were handed out in assembly. As proud pupils went to collect certificates for 50 metres, 100 metres, 200 metres and maybe even more, I was called up to receive a 'certificate of effort.' I could hear a curious hush fall upon the assembly hall. 'A certificate of effort'? This was a new one. What did that actually mean? Well, it meant I couldn't swim any of those above distances, in fact, I couldn't even swim 10 metres which was the minimum you had to do to receive a proper certificate. No, I couldn't swim at all, but I had shown effort. By effort, I presume they meant not actually drowning and thereby opening the school up to legal action. It was humiliating. People laughed as I cringed, the walk back to my seat seemed to take a lifetime. I haven't kept that certificate, but it did spur me on to learn to swim. I can do a whole 10 metres now.

Danny Robins, back row second from the right, outside West Jesmond School.

Danny Robins

Teenage kicks

Coming from Teesside it was a treat to spend a day in Newcastle. After getting off the train, the first pub I visited, aged 14, was the Forth. In those days it had two rooms, with pool on the right. My pal and I had committed the 'crime' of not buying our rail tickets before boarding the train; it was day one of the new 'open station system'. Having been fined most of our pocket money it seemed best to pay tribute to the city by drinking what was left.

The Haymarket was always the best destination for shopping. There was an antique centre in the old bus HQ, Attic near The Farmers and, Mecca for all dudes and dudettes, Handyside Arcade. Aside from the wonderful dingy boutiques, dodgy pet shop and Kard Bar we would 'explore' the unused upstairs and drink pomagne or sangria. It was compulsory to hang out at Volume Records before a coffee down the spiral staircase in the basement of the Bookhouse. I would return home with *Viz* and second-hand clothes from Fynd. I got into trouble once

Sarah Hall, 1984.

having bought a ticket for Nick Cave and the Bad Seeds at Tiffanys as I was only 15. Luckily my mother appreciated the significance of the gig and I was allowed to go.

Sarah Hall

As a young teenager, I would often take the bus to the city centre for a rendezvous with my friends. The ABC at the Haymarket was the venue for my first cinema visit without my parents. We watched *E.T.* from velveteen seats smelling of musky smoke. Kissing teenagers would go there to escape prying eyes. Much to my horror, a bout of laughter disturbed everyone's crying when someone secretly broke wind!

Eldon Garden, on the grave of the Handyside Arcade somehow doesn't give me the same awe I once felt. I have fond memories of the beautifully structured avenues of record shops, incense smells and hundreds of strange looking people meeting to compare the latest in hippy juice aroma. A sense of devilishness would enter me as I walked through this architectural monument, knowing that I was in a place where anything went; my mother always horrified that I had visited such a place when the smell of joss sticks drifted through the cracks of my bedroom door.

Tiffanys nightclub on New Bridge Street hosted under 16's disco nights. New Romantic haircuts and sullen faces with pale make-up and heavy eyeliner were everywhere as Culture Club and Human League blasted through the speakers.

Elaine McKenna

In the sixth form you were allowed to wear your own jackets instead of blazers over the green Church High uniform. My boyfriend used to meet me sometimes from school.

One day I was summoned to the headmistress's study. There were three lights outside of her room. Red to go away, amber to wait and green to come in – quite a scary experience, especially if you had done anything naughty. I'd recently been caught smoking in the toilets but wasn't aware of having done anything untoward since.

The head told me in no uncertain terms that I wasn't allowed to wear a leather bike jacket or ripped denim and that 'That punk rocker with the double mohican is not allowed to wait for you outside of school premises'! However, I was undeterred, I just used to meet him further down the street.

Karen Laidler

Karen Laidler

When we were in the sixth form at Walker School we had 'fun days'. On 9 April 1987 we took part in a fancy dress/sponsored activity day to raise money for the school which was on two different sites at the time. Sixth formers and teachers dressed up for the event. We decided to wear black and white, and to push a blackboard through the streets of Walker from one site to the other (presumably the school wanted it moved anyway).

Angela Merritt (née Wong), and Julie Hoggins

Slatyford Comprehensive, where I taught, was a large school with around 1,700 students and looked like a sprawling concrete blot. A special attraction was the huge swimming pool, a legacy of the T. Dan Smith days. It was challenging, with a real mixed intake, but it always had a buzz. We had a flourishing drama department and an orchestra.

Students either hated or supported you. I drove a mixture of old and newer cars, but my pride and joy was a Morgan. I was apprehensive leaving it in the car park but I needn't have worried, it was never touched. In fact one very snowy winter, a group of students volunteered to heave it out of the car park. Slatyford was a rough, tough place where you had to be straight with the students if you wanted them to respect you. Teaching poetry was something special there; students actually responded – of course it wasn't always positive!

I could never go shopping in Eldon Square without being accosted by my students … 'Hello Miss'. This particularly surprised a relative over from Australia; the lads in question looked rough, and could be, but their friendliness and nosiness meant that they had to be introduced.

One of the difficulties at Slatyford was the ongoing feud with John Marley school. One day, with nearly 250 John Marley students advancing across the field, a party of teachers drove their cars between the two camps and just about avoided a major disturbance.

My special memories involve the sixth form English groups. We were lucky to have the Gulbenkian Studio by the Playhouse, next to the University. When the RSC came up, the sixth form students were taken to as many shows there as possible; 50p and a cushion and we sat on the floor at the edge of the stage! They were immersed in Shakespeare and modern drama and that translated into exam success for many of our students and a change to their perspective on life. We also put on our own theatre productions; the most memorable for me was *Close the Coalhouse Door*. During our preparation for this we learned that Slatyford was actually built on the site of an old mine.

One day the whole building began to shake, the noise was deafening. Everyone, me included, rushed to the windows to see a Vulcan flying overhead, wonderful wingspan shape and utter filth spewing from its exhaust.

Maxine Patterson (née Bearne)

I was a Phillip Schofield fan. My sister and I went to see him in Edinburgh when he starred in *Joseph and his Technicolor Dreamcoat*. Imagine my delight when I found out he was going to be at the opening of the BBC Shop in Eldon Square! My next thought was what would I wear when we met?!! It would have to be something eye catching so he would notice me! At the time I made a lot of my own clothes, so I decided to wear a very colourful jumper that I had designed and knitted myself for a fashion show I was involved in through school. On 28 June 1988 I dragged my friend Julie along and we queued to see him. How excited I was! Phillip was very charming (I like to think he noticed me and my jumper) and Julie took a lovely photo of when we met. I wrote to Phillip and sent him the photo in the hope he would autograph and return it, and he did!

Angela Merritt (née Wong)

Angela Merritt

Peter Brabban

These signs in the photograph read:

NO CRUISE

RSC ACTORS SUPPORT GREENHAM WOMEN

THATCHER'S PRIORITIES AMAZE ME ....

RSC ACTORS SUPPORT GREENHAM WOMEN

"SAY "NO" TO CRUISE MISSILES

RSC ACTORS FOR PEACE

RSC ACTORS AGAINST THE BOMB

BETTER DEAD THAN ...

THE REAL ENEMY IS ALWAYS FEAR

These RSC actors took time off from perfomances at the Gulbenkian Studio and the Theatre Royal in 1983 to demonstrate against government policies at a Peace Camp outside St Thomas's Church opposite the Playhouse. They include Alun Armstrong and Sinnead Cusack.

The anti-CND protesters are from the Royal Grammar school on the same wintry day.

Peter Brabban

27

Our kids enjoyed visits to The Golden Hinde replica ship on the Quayside in March 1985. You could go on board and explore the cramped area below deck. The Tall Ships came in 1986 and the Quayside began to be somewhere you'd want to go to. (Anna Flowers)

Right, children learn the Green Cross Code at Walkergate School, 1986.

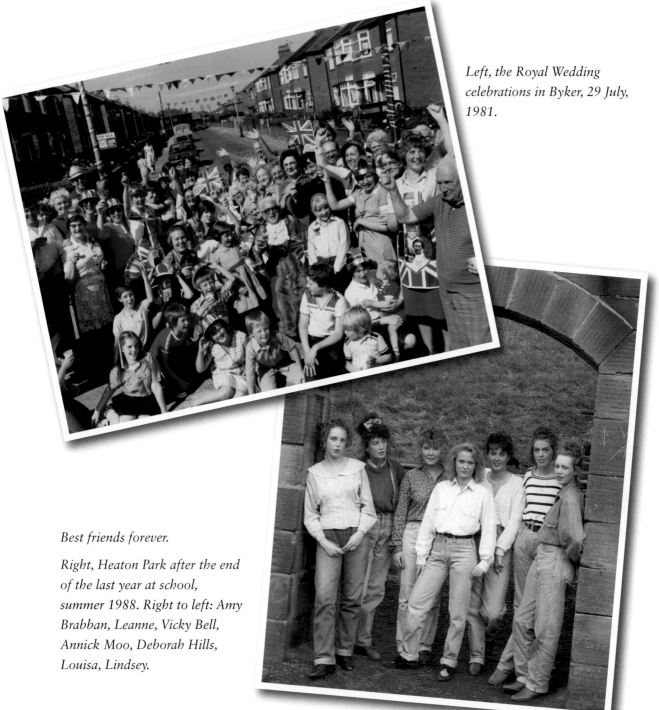

Left, the Royal Wedding celebrations in Byker, 29 July, 1981.

Best friends forever.

Right, Heaton Park after the end of the last year at school, summer 1988. Right to left: Amy Brabban, Leanne, Vicky Bell, Annick Moo, Deborah Hills, Louisa, Lindsey.

Books, books books

When Iris Penny opened the Bookhouse on Ridley Place in 1981 it was a revelation and a marvel as before this the only real bookshop had been Thorne's Student Bookshop on Percy Street. Good as Thorne's was, it was old fashioned. Iris Penny bought in an eclectic range of books, poetry, and art. And there was a lovely children's section run by the inspired Elisabeth Hammill (who later went to Waterstones when that opened in 1986 or 7). The atmosphere was relaxed and there was a (very crowded) coffee shop in the basement.

On 9 November 1985 we took our children to the second Northern Children's Book Festival at Eldon Square Recreation Centre. It was run by the children's section of the Central Library, and Elisabeth Hammill. Our daughter won *Lion at School* by Phillipa Pearce in the pop-up competition. Terry Jones was reading from *Eric the Viking* and *Nicobobinus* to our son's delight.

Anna Flowers

THE BOOKHOUSE

books – coffee
postcards
quick ordering
children's bookden

13 Ridley Place Newcastle-upon-Tyne tel(0632) 616128

THE NORTHERN CHILDREN'S BOOK FESTIVAL
SUPER SATURDAY!
7th November 1987 10 a.m. – 4.30 p.m.
Eldon Square Recreation Centre
Newcastle upon Tyne

FREE! ADMISSION

PETER CONNOLLY 11.15 & 2.15

Hundreds of Books for Sale!

Storyteller JAMES RIORDAN 10.15 & 1.15

JAN MARK 12.15 & 3.15

JAN PIENKOWSKI Join the Great Paint-In!

PANDORA'S PUPPET CIRCUS 12.00 & 3.00

Artist ALIKI 10.15 & 1.15

RUTH BROWN 12.15 & 3.15

FRANZ BRANDENBERG 11.15 & 2.15

POSTMAN PAT

MAKE A POP-UP with FRANKIE & MOIRA

Supported by Newcastle Festival

Further details at your local library

Children's Theatre

The 1980s was a great time for children's theatre and Newcastle had some of the best provision with companies such as Puppets and People, Bruvvers and Skin and Bones writing and performing plays aimed at entertaining and educating young people. There were grants a-plenty to pay for it all too.

As a teacher at Cruddas Park Nursery School I worked on a 'don't talk to strangers' project with one such group. They transposed the story of *Little Red Riding Hood* into a story of a small child living on the Cruddas Park Estate. At the end they asked one small boy what lesson he had learnt to which he replied 'I know I must never talk to strange wolves.' Hmmm!! Maybe the message was a bit too subtle for three-year-olds!

Living in Heaton, our own children grew up with regular theatrical experiences. The University Theatre began to offer a variety of children's arts on Saturdays and we went to see Johnny Morris telling his animal stories, *Tubby the Tuba* performed by the Northern Sinfonia, and a wonderful production of *Angelina* complete with tightrope walking and circus acrobatics.

The same theatre changed the face of Christmas family entertainment forever by dropping traditional pantomime in favour of spectacular shows like *The Pirate Queen*, *The Ice Queen* and *Beauty and the Beast*.

Annie Moir

Top, enthralled by puppet theatre at St Georges's Fete, May 1984.

Anthony Flowers

The Adventures Of Red Riding Hood

By the mid-1980s, the teaching staff at West Jesmond were involved in working to rule. Because they refused to supervise lunchtimes, we working parents were forced to organise voluntary lunch clubs in church halls, and, for Heaton Manor pupils, at the People's Theatre. Some sessions were held in Jesmond Parish Church hall for a while, and I remember rushing from work on my bike in all weathers to supervise and help out, often arriving dripping and freezing. All after school activities were suspended and many never really recovered. My son was heartbroken that his school football team stopped playing, and all the musical and craft activities disappeared.

Fiona Clarke

We were struggling to pay the mortgage by the early 1980s ... but just a few years earlier we had been able to buy our large terrace house in Jesmond on a teacher's salary. My earnings weren't taken into account. There was no money to spare as interest rates zoomed ever upwards. In 1982 we couldn't afford to repair the car so my husband had to resort to the bus to get to his school in West Denton. We walked or cycled. There was dry rot, rising damp, and a leaky roof, lining paper on the living room floor, but I loved living in Jesmond; there were young families, toddler groups, street parties, and Jesmond Dene nearby. There was Mandala down the road for wholefoods, Laws Stores on Acorn Road, and Presto in Heaton, which seemed quite impressive. The 33 bus ran regularly to the city centre, and the Metro from West Jesmond would whisk a huge second-hand Silver Cross pram into town (if you could afford a ticket). Our babysitting circle ran on paperclips (it cost you more after 11pm).

Chernobyl worried the kids (and us) when that happened. They were anxious about drinking milk.

Anna Flowers

Anna Flowers

A street party in Queens Road, Jesmond, 1981.

In July 1982, after almost eight years on the housing list, we were given the keys to a brand new council house in St Michael's Mount, Byker. Our two-bedroom flat in Commercial Road was bursting at the seams after the birth, in 1980, of our third baby, Gareth so we were looking forward to a bit more space.

The view from the upside down house, 1982.

The day we went to view our new home was so exciting. I can remember opening the front door and being slightly perplexed as there was a flight of stairs going up and a flight going down! Downstairs there was a lovely kitchen and dining room and two bedrooms. The stairs led up to a large sitting room with a huge picture window and a view of the Tyne Bridge and most of Newcastle. There was also a third bedroom and bathroom on this floor.

The day we moved in I managed to put net curtains up but the other curtains would have to wait. Most of the estate seemed to move in on the same day so there were a lot of vans and removal men milling around and new neighbours to meet. Our youngest child, who was two years old, slept in his first bed and insisted he was a big boy and threw his dummy in the bin. I expected a sleepless night but he was fine until there was an almighty thunderstorm. One by one there was a knock on our bedroom door. We ended up, all five of us, in our bed – so much for more room.

Living in an upside down house as the kids called it could be difficult; you had to have eyes in the back of your head with so many stairs. I spent most of my time in the kitchen-dining room and only used the living room in the evenings or I would have been constantly running up and down the stairs.

There were lots of young families and the older children had more freedom as there was only one road and the majority of the estate was traffic free. We lived there for 14 years and the upside down house had many special happy memories as it was the place our family grew up.

Lynn Steele

LET'S DANCE

David Bowie, 1983

Out on the town

I'd discovered beer, pubs and girls. I even had a job during my year out from college. It was in Gateshead, and since the Metro hadn't extended that far and the Gateshead interchange not yet opened, I had to catch two buses just to get across the river.

At lunchtime, we would sometimes go to the Trafalgar in West Street. Often there would be an old bloke in the corner who would start whistling bird calls after a couple of beers. Even though one of the region's first kebab shops had recently opened across the road (with a choice of chips or salad to accompany your kebab – how's that for haute cuisine?), I realised fairly quickly that this was probably not the best place to find young ladies on a Friday night.

Then we discovered Pumphreys – or more specifically Rick's Bar in the Cloth Market. It was one of the first places in town to have a Happy Hour. Essentially buy one get

The Groat Market, 1988. Haute cuisine?

Northumberland Street, Christmas 1986.

Friday night was always boys' night out; we met locally then at around 7pm jumped in taxis and headed for the town. We went from pub to pub regardless of the weather (I assume it's still the same) and usually ended up at the Cordwainers, packed like sardines. That was where I met my wife actually. (Dale Toothill)

one free, we cared not that the normal price of one was probably twice as much as the bar in the Trafalgar; this was 'the' place to be between half five and half six. The promotion was to be copied by most of the bars in town over the coming years, as places elsewhere gradually raised their game (and their prices), rebranded with a new name, usually ending in 's', and invested in some disco lighting and cocktail umbrellas.

Roland Finch

Rick's Cocktail Bar, 1985.

We went to Butler's disco, and the Cordwainers, the Pineapple, Masters and Rick's wine bar, Presidents, Nicky's, or Tux 2 and Manhattan near the library. We'd go to the Studio at the Oxford Galleries; you'd get free tickets on your birthday. There was Tiffanys at the Oxford too. It had the same clientèle as the Mayfair.

Sharon Reeve

Tuxedo was the 'top venue' in the early 1980s; the first sophisticated, London-style club in Newcastle. It was owned by Michael Quadrini, who also had the *Tuxedo Princess* (two different boats over several years) moored on the Gateshead side of the Tyne near the Tyne Bridge. DJs at Tuxedo Junction included Big Phil.

Each of the booth tables had telephones so that you could phone another table and chat up someone you fancied – not the tables to use if with your partner! There were also often male or female pole and cage dancers on the raised platform next to the dance floor. This was the club to be seen at during the late 1970s and early 1980s with your padded shoulders and 'big hair'.

Christopher Baglee

THE MOST LAVISH NIGHTSPOT IN THE COUNTRY
BAMBURGH HOUSE, MARKET STREET, NEWCASTLE UPON TYNE.
Telephone (0632) 23211 or 23238

We couldn't afford to go to Tuxedo Junction regularly; we may have been half a dozen times, sometimes catching what might have been the 2.25am (Sunday morning) train from Newcastle Central Station to Whitley Bay to get home.

I think there was just one dance floor to start with, but eventually you could walk through to Grand Central and then onto a third area (I cannot remember the name but it had a 'tropical theme'). Part of the connecting area had multi-coloured lights on the ceiling and in the darkness it looked like hundreds of intensely coloured stars.

People we knew thought of Tuxedo Junction as a 'high end' establishment for the better-off, but it was accessible (only just) to the likes of 'us'. I remember that just to the left of the entrance was the restaurant, separated from the dance floor by glass panels with vertical rows of small white fairy lights. This was the sit-down restaurant; diners had bottles of champagne; I may have been able to get into Tuxedo Junction – but that was a step too high for me.

To the right of the restaurant was an oval dance floor surrounded by a single ring of tables – each of which had a telephone so you could make contact with someone who may have caught your eye. A great idea, but if your girlfriend received a call, it could lead to a little disagreement! A few steps up were more tables and there was a bar at each end of the room. Two bars in one area – that was extravagance!

Allan Finlay

Allan Finlay

Allan Finlay

THE MOST LAVISH NIGHTSPOTS IN THE COUNTRY

MINI MENU

Allan and pals on a night out, November 1986. They were perhaps NOT at Tuxedo Junction!

The Boat

The floating disco, *Tuxedo Princess*, was a big thing. It was a new experience and a huge change from the smoky dark night clubs of Newcastle. The students were great fans although there were one or two 'overboard' incidents and it was reckoned that despite the smart appearance of the *Tuxedo* staff (in naval gear) they were pretty tough with unruly clients and drunks.

Hélène Dolder

Tuxedo Princess in all her splendour, 1984.

I only ever went on the *Tuxedo Princess* once, and that was an experience! I don't know if I just picked a bad night, but it seemed to be listing very badly and going on the dance floor was like climbing a hill! Even at that time I remember thinking this could be quite dangerous as people had had a bit to drink and it was just a small dance floor, so they were lurching out onto the decks. I can't remember any security people being around. So I thought it was a bit risky but I never heard of anyone falling in.

Kath Cassidy

Anyone who's seen the movie *Stormy Monday*, filmed in Newcastle in 1987, and starring Sting and Melanie Griffith, will notice that at the time the Quayside was a pretty grim place. But that didn't stop us flocking to 'The Boat', or more correctly, the *Tuxedo Princess*, which opened for business in 1983, with its staff dressed as sailors and its revolving dance floor. It was an extension of Tuxedo Junction which featured telephones on each table and, on more than one occasion, a 'wet t-shirt' competition. I do remember the wall mounted TVs. The first pub video jukebox didn't appear until a couple of years later, and with a screen at head height was almost pointless if the place was busy. But the ones in 'Tux' were much higher so a complete novelty, although strangely my enduring memory of the place is not a pop video, but one night in November 1980 watching Sugar Ray Leonard demolish Roberto Duran to regain the world middleweight boxing championship.

Roland Finch

I was there for the opening night of the *Tuxedo Princess*. My best mate Tony Knox was manager so I was invited to the champagne (VIP) opening. It was fun when it opened, completely different. It was new and pristine when it arrived though over a period of time it fell into decline. At that time when I was a young and impressionable 20 year old, it was all great fun. It was mainly disco, but live bands played in various rooms. I played at a private party there with the East Side Torpedoes.

Steve Dolder

Brendan Thorpe

In my early days of going clubbing in Newcastle I spent many a happy (drunken?) night in Casablanca, near the Haymarket bus station. We all were very excited when the rumours of a new club began to circulate. Rockshots, on Waterloo Street, was opened by the team who had run the Casablanca and was much glitzier than its predecessor. I remember the opening night with a true star of the small screen – Pat Phoenix, our very own Elsie Tanner from *Coronation Street*. Loudly patterned, low cut evening dress, big gold jewellery – every inch a star. She was with her long-term partner, Antony Booth, now better knows as Cherie Blair's father. We all queued to get a chance to speak to her and get her to autograph a photo. The following night there was a celebrity cabaret – Su Pollard. The cabaret got even better over the years; Sylvester, Divine and Eartha Kitt were just a few of the stars!

Brendan Thorpe

The gay clubs were always popular with people like me who wanted a friendly night out and good music. The Casablanca above the Haymarket – a former news cinema – was brilliant in its day. Rockshots, in Waterloo Street was another place I'd go. They had 'straight nights' on a Thursday.

Chris Donald

Top, Brendan ready for Rockshots.
Right, Brendan's autographed photo of Pat Phoenix.

The Mayfair

There were few bearable options for post-pub drinking in the late 80s; most clubs offered Stock, Aitken and Waterman disco or pensioner sleaze at Greys. We used to go to the Mayfair. Rock Nite occupied the main venue but we would go to the side room that hosted The Drop. The area was done out with draped sheets hanging from the ceiling and walls that made you feel as if you were in an over-relaxed tent. I seem to remember cushions on the floor. The overall memory is a sea of crusties, dreadlocks, tie dye, fragrant smoke, a dub, bassy soundtrack and falling asleep.

The Drop, above, was a reggae club in one of the Mayfair's small function rooms on Fridays, started at the end of the eighties by the lads who ran Heartbreak Soup on the Quayside. There was also a Goth/punk club called the Gear Box in the next room. Once you'd paid your entrance money you were free to roam between the two, but we'd often sit on the balcony in the main ballroom watching the heavy metal fans go through their manoeuvres on the dancefloor below. When the Mayfair was full to capacity, this was one of the great cultural spectacles of northern Europe. (Marshall Hall)

The bar supplied expensive watery McEwan's lager. It was impossible to get any tipsiness from this so it is no wonder that intoxicants took an alternative form, be it via hipflask or pipe.

I once wandered into the rock room, a mass of air guitaring and hair. My request to the DJ for some Hawkwind was met with, 'Sorry pet, that will die on its arse'!

Sarah Hall

Heavy metal group R & B Spitfires perform at the Mayfair Ballroom during the Sunday Sun Night of Rock in aid of the Charlie Bear Scanner Appeal, 6 November 1981.

I remember the Mayfair! It was our favourite. We'd get the all night bus home after. We saw the Tygers of Pan Tang but it was mostly just a disco. We'd go every Friday night. When we got in the house we'd have Marks & Spencer Swiss Roll and Viennese Whirls to eat.

Barbara Bravey

I went to the Mayfair every Thursday from the age of 14 and danced nonstop for four hours. Thursday was Indie night … Anti-Pop I think it was called! My sister took me there for my 14th birthday to see Jesus and Mary Chain. It was big and hot … Goths standing round looking miserable and sweaty and worrying about their hair flopping. It was a really fantastic experience and I went to more and more gigs after that. My sister got me in every Thursday until they shut it when I was 17, when I had to start going to the Rock Nites. The deal was I had to stay awake at school the next day.

The Sugar Cubes were due to play one Thursday night so I didn't go, of course, as they weren't cool enough, but then they cancelled at the last minute and played another Thursday, so that was two Thursdays ruined!

Kemi Kilburn

In the mid 80s I sang with a band called the Immortals. I can't sing, but they said just do your sexy dance. Once at the Mayfair they turned my microphone off so I couldn't be heard. I was tone deaf! Most of my boyfriends were in a band, there were so many bands! I was always going to see bands.

Karen Laidler

Walkers Club opened in the old Dolce Vita. It was pretty up-market when it first opened, a bar area downstairs, which was open for lunch, and a night club upstairs. I remember Duran Duran having a private party there one night. I do recall travelling down to Whitley Bay on a Saturday evening; local lad Andy Taylor from Duran Duran had some interest in bar called Rio I believe, and Sting's brother had a place called Dune that was popular for a while.

Dale Toothill

Greys Club was a club that from the start was really for the over 30s, sophisticated. We had a dress code, no jeans, collar and tie … it relaxed a bit later. I caused a bit of controversy. I saw women drinking pints so I went up to them and told them that I'd prefer to see them drinking two halves, for the same price as a pint of course. Nobody was keen on seeing women drinking a pint. We were a bit old fashioned, and nobody minded. It sounds strange now.

We would get detectives coming in after their duties. It was convenient for Pilgrim Street and it was nice for them to relax and not meet any gangsters or be pestered. We had no drug scene, the only time was when someone smoked a joint in the gents and Tommy went in and sorted that out. Never anything else. They used to say it was 'grab a granny' night at Greys and I told them to just enjoy it. We weren't involved with other clubs. We were the only club doing live music, the others were all disco, and we ran disco by the end of the 80s.

David Macbeth

Bars only stayed open till 10.30pm, so after that people tended to go on to night clubs. I went to Julies, which was really popular and full of movers and shakers but I didn't love it myself. I preferred the Cooperage which was more hippyish but still had a nice atmosphere.

I used to go to the Barn on Leazes Park Road, which was totally mad with a big stuffed bear inside the door, chandeliers and 1930s music. The people were eccentric. I also liked the Stage Door on Stowell Street. It was very friendly and family run. The owner's wife would take the ticket money and there was a bar with a disco downstairs. I liked it as you could dance and have a drink or sit and talk upstairs with the jukebox which played good music. You got to

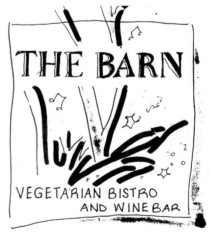

THE BARN

VEGETARIAN BISTRO AND WINE BAR

OPEN 11 AM TO 12:30 AFTER MIDNIGHT
LATE LICENCE
MONDAY TO SATURDAY

know people and it was a safe club with a wide age range. We used to get taxis home.

By the mid 1980s we tended to have a drink in Jesmond first. Osborne road was starting to have a few places like Trotters wine bar with Italian restaurant. Or we'd go to the Brandling or Collingwood, or the Carriage. Themed pubs were a big thing. The Carriage was near the railway and was popular and you could walk into town from there. People would stand outside Trotters in freezing weather – it was a bit of a posers' place. No outdoor heaters then of course.

Kath Cassidy

The Carriage, 1982. It occupied the old Jesmond railway station, and a novelty feature was the old railway carriage.

Going out to Julies nightclub was what we revolved around. When my friend Julie and I were moving to America we had a Julie and Julie's Going away party at Julies in 1984.

Julie Sloan

You are invited to
JULIE AND JULIE'S GOING AWAY PARTY
Thurs. 1st Nov.

★ The best music
★ High standard of clientele
★ Dress casual but smart
★ Open Tues - Wed - Thurs - Fri - Sat 10 pm - 2 am
★ Parties catered for (any occasion) from 2 to 250

The management reserves the right to refuse admission

PARTY

Julies '84
Quayside, Newcastle. Tel: 327240

Alternatively ...

I was 17 in 1980 and still at school but in the evenings I went to the Senate bar, one of the few alternative bars in Newcastle. It later became Luckies. In early 80s there was a very gay bar at the front end, and at the back it was all punks and alternative people. You'd meet your friends in the Senate, or in later years the Broken Doll. You'd call at the Percy Arms which was a bikers' pub. The Doll attracted a great mix of people, and everyone was welcome. There were lots of bands playing upstairs and pool tables. Then we'd go to a club. How did I get out every night, go to college and hold down two jobs?

Karen Laidler

This was at a time when you were turned away from clubs and pubs for wearing a studded belt or wristband. There were relatively few places for punks/hippies or anyone slightly different. The Jubilee was the only rock bar.

There was the Delby around the corner from the Mayfair on Low Friar Street. On a Saturday night it became very alternative, a real dive. The floor was wet and sticky from spilt drinks but we loved it. I've never seen such an eclectic mix of people. It was above the Dolce Vita and cost £1 to get in. One night there was a fire and we had to be evacuated. It only ran for a year or so 1980-81.

After the pub we'd all go to the Mayfair, which had an alternative night. You had to pay an old penny to get in

FUTURIST DISCO
AT THE DELBY
10th APRIL   9 p.m
£1 ON DOOR   2 a.m.

and a new penny to buy a pint. Also there was Rockshots which did alternative nights on Tuesdays and Thursdays. We were limited as to where we could go.

When I went to see the Cramps at the Mayfair some people were doing the Chicken dance and because I was quite small, I got pushed right to the front, not a very nice experience. I lost both my shoes in the melée and my brothers only got one back for me … what happened to that other red stiletto?

There were many little clubs that came and went. One was the Junction on Northumberland Street. It was upstairs, above the shops. In those days clubs had to serve food in order to get a licence, though nobody wanted food at 11pm. It was another place to go when the pubs shut. Most of these places only survived for around a year. There was also the North Eastern near Worswick Street bus station. They did pie and chips. These clubs were all £1 to get in. The Jewish Mother did food so they could stay open too.

We liked reggae so on a Sunday night we went to the Barley Mow on City Road to hear the DJ. That was a favourite place. The first room was cosy with an open fire, and there were other rooms. It later became all open plan and lost the atmosphere. We'd also go to a blues club in the west end.

Karen Laidler

Ridicule is nothing to be scared of

There was no point trying to get into a nightclub in the early eighties if your wardrobe differed from the norm, and the norm, as defined by a bouncer, was black slacks and loafers, preferably accessorised with a skinny tie and white socks. Any deviation from this and you were strongly and often violently advised to stand aside, so that the long queues of bequiffed blokes and bubble-permed beauties could be rushed through instead.

When the post-punk era dawned on Newcastle around 1980, an alternative to this scene emerged. A group of us gathered to enjoy our individuality in the back room of the Senate, a gay bar opposite the Civic Centre, where anyone or indeed anything that differed from the norm was more than welcome. Unlike the rest of Newcastle, nobody batted an eyelid at people with hilarious hairstyles who were decked out in apparently random combinations of studded bike jackets, ball gowns, cocktail suits and ripped jeans, or

Karen and boyfriend, Affaz, at the Casablanca, November 1982, and, below, in the Baltic Tavern on the Quayside after The Tube.

lads nipping into the ladies' to touch up their eyeliner.

Saturday nights at the Senate were best finished off with the trip to the Delby, and at closing time we'd form up into a convoy for safety's sake before making the long journey across town to the club. Even though we were often 30 or 40 strong, bevvied-up passers-by were riled enough by this spectacle to run up and kick lumps out of us, all the way down Northumberland Street. Many simply took a taxi from home straight to the club; being so exotic they could only survive in their bedrooms or the Delby.

The club was above La Dolce Vita, on Low Friar Street, and we'd walk up several flights of stairs where the promoter's Mam vetted the clientèle and took our entrance money. The room looked as though it hadn't been used in decades, so it provided a splendidly bleak and sleazy backdrop for the mix of punk, industrial, electronic, reggae and Northern Soul music; and those who gathered to enjoy it. On the downside, the plumbing was knackered so you were always ankle-deep in urine in the gents', while dodging the occasional fist coming through the wall from the adjacent ladies'. But nobody

Mike Atherfold (Affaz) differing from the norm, Fenham, around 1982.

cared, because everyone knew each other and it was literally the only place in town we could be. And for this reason, it remains my favourite club ever.

I was there the night the fire brigade burst through the door, urging us to get out of the building immediately. Nobody had noticed the smoke, and more importantly, they didn't want to leave their drinks. When everyone was finally dragged out of the club, there were some bruising encounters on the street with the knucklehead evacuees from the Dolcey downstairs where the fire had started, and that was pretty much the end of the Delby.

But the notion of an 'alternative scene' had taken hold, and by 1982 'alternative nights' were becoming a common feature across town, in disused nightclub bars, backrooms of pubs, snooker joints, and hotel ballrooms. In 1984, Shaun Wilson and Ray Callan established the magnificently cool Mr M's

Marshall Hall having fun at M's club around 1984.

THE LEGENDARY M's CLUB

held in TIFFANYS BAMBOO ROOM

BLUES, 60s SOUL, JAZZ, FUNK, WITH A TOUCH OF REGGAE & OTHER SURPRISING THINGS

10·00 till 2·00 EVERY FRIDAY

on Fridays in the Bamboo Suite at Tiffanys – the very heart of black slacks/white sock territory – and were cramming around five or six hundred people into a room licensed to hold half that number.

Fashions changed far more quickly back then, and by the mid-point of the decade most of the pioneers of the scene from the Senate and the Delby had tweaked their clothes and attitudes accordingly. But many remained as punks or evolved into Goths with their own niche club nights, while those who refused to adapt were confined eternally to their bedrooms. The general public also became more tolerant of people who didn't conform to the fashions of the day, and it became possible to walk around town of an evening relatively unmolested, as the line between 'alternative' and 'normal' gradually blurred.

By the time Riverside opened in 1985, providing a permanent home for thousands of members who felt no part of Newcastle's mainstream nightlife – indeed, Riv's doormen turned people away – people who looked too 'normal' – there wasn't really any point describing the scene as 'alternative', in the sense it was originally intended.

Which is a massive shame, because it marked the last time that young people would shock and disturb ordinary folk: something that had happened for three decades, and that I had grown up believing we were honour-bound to do.

Marshall Hall

Top, just hanging out (for a fashion photo shoot) at the West Road cemetery, 1982.

Left, a more mainstream gathering, at Lazers bar, Grey Street, 1988. Lazers wine bar featured Newcastle's first laser show: a single beam of green light that bounced around the walls off a small mirror ball. This thrilling spectacle was viewed with both awe and a slight apprehension that it'd have somebody's eye out! (Marshall Hall)

52

The Broken Doll

I had a job as a barmaid at the Broken Doll on Blenheim Street. We had so many parties there. Although I was working I knew everyone. There was a great atmosphere, and everyone got along, skinheads, heavy metal people, punk rockers, hippies and bikers. There was an upstairs where bands played, and on Sundays and bank holidays there would also be bands on like Dan to Dan and Big Ray and the Hipthrusters downstairs. Despite several 'Save the Doll' party nights. It was knocked down in the late 80s to make way for St James Boulevard.

Karen Laidler

Club Trevor

The Broken Doll was the place where the disenfranchised tribes of Newcastle met, although that sounds a bit poncey. It was always full of a mix of punks, bikers, assorted musos and old blues blokes, gaggles of drunken girls from private schools and an assortment of very shady people just generally going about their shady business. In a word, magnificent …

Live
BLUES * JAZZ
ROCK
GOOD FOOD
AVAILABLE
SPECIAL CHEAP
DOUBLES
AT ALL TIMES

CLASSIC
JUKE BOX

EVERYTHING IS
NOT WHAT
IT SEEMS

the BLUES SESSION
BROKEN DOLL,
BLENHEIM STREET,
NEWCASTLE

As well as being a multi-purpose den of iniquity, the Doll was a great live venue. It had two stages, the downstairs one was more blues-based and attracted a slightly older crowd, while the upstairs room hosted pretty much everything else. It was free to hire this upstairs room, which gave a massive leg-up to loads of local bands and promoters; all you had to do was book an evening, print some posters, sort out a PA system for the bands and you had yourself a gig. The Doll's management didn't even want a slice of the door take, so you got to keep 100 per cent of whatever you made. Inspired by this, I started my own monthly local bands night called Club Trevor. For reasons lost to the mists of time, I decided that, if you could provide ID that proved that your first name was Trevor, you got in for free. This offer was taken up by Newcastle's Trevor community, and every night I held the club there at least two or three blokes called Trev turned up, demanding to be let in for nothing.

Ettrick Scott

Scenes at the Broken Doll.

My favourite Doll moment would have to be the time that laughable US shock-rockers Christian Death turned up to play the venue in a tour bus that would have probably held more people than the room they were gigging in. They looked totally horrified, but put on the full show anyway, using radio microphones and smoke machines in a room where they had to shift the pool table to one side to get the audience in. It was hilarious; pure Spinal Tap comes to Newcastle.

Ettrick Scott

Students, from the nearby School of Music at the College of Arts and Technology, at the Broken Doll, around 1986. The rest of us were probably inside the pub drinking Slalom lager. The poster in the window advertises The Fabulous Roadrunners. Other bands I remember at the Doll from that era include (I think) Death by Milk Float, The Sensible Pencils, Tea Dance Myth and Jacques Giraffe. (Andy Clark)

For you this Bank Holiday Weekend live at the

BROKEN DOLL

* Friday 24th. *
CHINA DRUM

* Saturday 25th. *
CLUB TREVOR

* Sunday 26th. *
(a.m.)   THE LEAPIN' LIZARDS

(p.m.)   ROGER HIGGINS
BOTTLE NECK BOOGIE BAND

(upstairs)   THE EXCHANGE CLUB

* Monday 27th. *
(a.m.)   THE HIPTHRUSTERS

(p.m.)   DAN to DAN

(upstairs)   STATE OF SHOCK

Dark shoddy rooms and familiar faces

Newcastle was bleak in the 1980s. Unemployment was high. Culture was low. The town centre was deserted on weekday nights and if you did venture out, you had to be wary, particularly if you had a look that wasn't to everybody's taste. There will always be knackers looking for a fight, but conditions then – the quiet, unobserved streets – were much in their favour.

From nowhere it seemed, although probably owing a debt to the DIY spirit of the recent punk movement, an alternative club scene developed that didn't impose dress codes to stop you at the door and send you scuttling home. Suddenly there were places where it felt good to be dressed up and you could meet people you liked the look of. There were places to go where you could enjoy the music you already liked and discover more besides. These were exciting and liberating nights. They were not student nights and pre-dated a strategy of chasing the student pound. They were nights for local people by local people. Occasionally, a small group of students would come down from the Poly, and that was immediately evident. Nudge, nudge 'They're from the Poly,' but said more with curiosity than resentment.

At first the alternative scene was founded upon the tolerance of the gay venues. The regulars at the Senate Bar and the Casablanca Club were mainly welcoming and certainly curious about the strange looking creatures that began to take up residence in the corners.

Ros Seymour

Simon McKay on Northumberland Street, mid 1980s. The trench coat was quite stylish. They sold similar ones, in green, in Handyside Arcade, but this grey one cost 20p at a jumble sale.

Club nights were destined to appear in the dingy rooms where nobody else wanted to be, or in decent rooms on the weekday nights when nobody else wanted them. Probably the first major alternative club of the decade was at the Delby on Low Friar Street. Tony Porter, a Saturday night regular, recalls crunching his way across the broken glass on the floors and the foul toilets. He remembers guys using the ladies' toilet as 'it was the only one with a mirror [where] they could re-do their make up!'

Simon McKay

Simon and friends at the Senate Bar, May 1982.

The Senate was an eclectic mix of gay and alternatives, don't know how it worked, but it did, both Balmbras and the Senate bar had the distinctive flock wallpaper look, a great way of identifying these locations in photographs from this period. (Mike Atherfold)

My first experience of this emerging scene was the backroom at Balmbras on a Saturday night. I was impressed by how central music was to the night. There was no obvious dance floor, but I do recall there being some dancing towards the end of the night (which was at 11pm). The music was always brand new, except for Bowie but he was regarded as contemporary. There are no horror stories about the toilets in Balmbras, but what was the rodent situation? In early 1982 when the New Romantic Movement was at its height in Newcastle (maybe there were 30 or so obvious converts in the region), I remember a girl, strutting about in a long white dress. She was heavily made up and had long blonde hair backcombed mercilessly and piled high on her head. The word got around that she had brought her pet mouse with her and it was in her hair – she was wearing it!

The scene was small and connected. Flyers and posters appeared at the Senate Bar for a new night at

Tiffanys on a Wednesday called 'A Packet of Cornflakes'. We all went. The music was diverse and drew upon the past. As well as contemporary music there were old soul and jazz records mixed in ... even Marilyn Monroe! I can still remember some of the people that would rush excitedly to the floor when their favourite record came on. Of course you can guess who the B52 girls favoured! There were two of them and could have passed for sisters – both had blonde hair and wore carefully co-ordinated clothes. They were very controlled in their movements particularly on the dance floor where they were almost static. They would simply look down to one side and do nothing more than raise and lower their forearms. They were just as economical in their speech (friendly, but far from verbose). It occurs to me now that they were probably very shy, but at the time they just seemed so cool.

On Sunday nights, there was the Downbeat Club in the Collingwood pub on High Bridge. This was strictly a reggae night and attracted a knowledgeable crowd of regulars. Other weekend nights came and went – The Junction (on Northumberland Street, up the stairs next to Callers) and the North Eastern Hotel on Carliol Square. Meanwhile, Tiffanys expanded its reach, launching Mr M's on a Friday night. This was a breakthrough point – a decent room on a popular night and this is probably where the student scene began in Newcastle – it attracted groups of students in droves. Suddenly the room became packed with an ever-changing cast. The alternative club scene was shifting quickly, the spirit would continue for a while at least in quieter nights attended by a smaller but dedicated crowd – The Monday Club at Tiffanys and The Redhaus at the Redhouse on a Saturday.

The changes came thick and fast. By the mid-80s, Tiffanys was less important and Rockshots become the new Mecca. For a while, it continued very much in the spirit of previous alternative nights. By now, the students had become a much larger percentage of the regular clientèle and were now actively courted by the clubs. The real 80s had arrived. Separateness was no longer celebrated. The aim was to appeal to as many people as possible and generate large quantities of money. I continued to go to the clubs throughout the 80s, but they became very different places. Perhaps it was my bias for the years in which I came of age, but I missed the naivety and intimacy that had gone before. By now, big with

Tiffanys, New Bridge Street, 1982.
At Tiffanys there were different nights for different kinds of music. It was rock night on a Monday. It was more
trendy at the weekend and more alternative during the week. Tiffs showcased more local bands like Raven, who
became massive in the USA, Hellenbach and Emerson. (Nicola Booth)

bright lights was essential.

I remember the Royal Wedding and Live Aid of course, but my most meaningful memories of the 80s occurred in the years exactly between those events. My memories are set in dark, shoddy rooms visited each week by familiar faces. These are memories so potent I can still feel the energy and the atmosphere created by the people in these rooms. But then why wouldn't I? I was actually there. These are memories of something I was part of and not something I spent the day watching on TV!

Simon McKay

Simon McKay published the Newcastle music magazine Eccentric Sleeve Notes 1981-84 (now available online) and was a club DJ 1983-89. He currently presents a weekly radio show called Post Punk Britain.
www.eccentricsleevenotes.com

The Leaf Room at Tiffanys. This was the Monday Club, 1985.

I guess my 80s experiences started with the dawning of the New Romantic movement. I was 16 in 1980, and in awe of the colourful fashions and creativity of the scene. I bought a synthesizer and joined a couple of bands: Abante Rhythm and Expo Mosaic. Expo's first gig was at Balmbras, the place to be for the emerging alternative scene. Big Mick (*right*) was the DJ at Balmbras and one of the singers for Expo Mosaic.

Mike Atherfold

The legendary Riverside

The seeds of what was to become the legendary Riverside music venue were sown in early 1982 when Newcastle City Council set up a series of workshops for local bands and others interested in music to develop the moribund music scene in the city. A series of music collectives from across Tyneside, harnessing the energy of youth, engaged with the initiative and a group known as Metropolis, headed by Keith Jeffrey (later to be known as 'Mr Riverside' due to his dedication to the project), investigated funding opportunities for a new independent music venue in Newcastle.

The first draft of a business plan was written on the back of Keith's A-level Biology book and an application was made to the City Council for £250,000 in Inner City Partnership funding; the fund had been set up by Margaret Thatcher's Conservative Government as part of a range of policies to address urban decay and social unrest in the aftermath of the riots a year earlier. A petition was started and members of Metropolis even travelled to London to obtain the signatures of a wide variety of entertainment luminaries, including John Peel, George Martin, David 'Kid' Jensen and the actor Christopher Timothy. The momentum continued as various independent music venues across the UK were visited, including the Leadmill in Sheffield and the Zap Club in Brighton.

In September 1982 a new collective was formed called Lula Music (named after the Gene Vincent song, *Be Bop A Lula*), which was a merger of Metropolis and another youth club based collective known as Band Aid. Lula Music was described as a 'self-help group for musicians' and was run as a strict collective with an ethos of

A meeting of minds at the Central Library, around 1985.

equality and a burning desire to make Newcastle a better place through a vibrant cultural renaissance. Eventually a grant of £120,000 was offered by the City Council, short of the amount planned for but enough to keep the dream alive. Further money was raised through the release of an EP and a series of small fundraising gigs involving local bands.

During 1983 and through 1984 the collective continued to meet regularly as a building was sought to transform into the city's new music venue and cultural hub. One night in November 1984, as Keith Jeffrey was

Rik Walton

Members outside the Riverside building, 1985.

walking from Manors Metro Station to the Barley Mow pub on the Quayside he spotted the old Mawson, Swan and Morgan print works warehouse on Melbourne Street. The building was the right size, in the right location and above all relatively cheap. At this stage the NRCDA (Northern Regional Co-operative Development Agency), which included Riverside's later Director Andy Balman, assisted the collective with advice and support, including a feasibility study.

Lula Music became a co-operative called Riverside Entertainments Ltd and regular, well attended meetings with various interested parties started at the Central Library. In January 1985 the building was bought for £42,000 and work began to transform a dusty old printer's warehouse into an exciting new music venue and cultural hub.

Eventually, on 13 June 1985, Riverside opened and what started out as nothing more than an idealistic vision drafted on the back of a school exercise book became a reality and went on to become a legendary, world renowned music venue right here in Newcastle upon Tyne.

Carl Taylor

For information about the book, 'Riverside: Newcastle's Legendary Alternative Music Venue' by Hazel Plater & Carl Taylor visit hazelplater.com. You will also find info on a forthcoming documentary film about the venue.

Riverside was the best venue ever! We were (and still are) shareholders of this members' only club. There were times when there were too many good gigs in one week to afford (I missed Nirvana for this reason).

We would drink Slalom D lager in the Broken Doll before taking the Metro to Manors from Central Station. Once there I would smuggle cans of Kestrel super in my tights (resulting in a most ungainly, yet frisk proof, gait). I once trapped myself in one of the old cinema seats by demonstrating how it could tip up with me inside. I think that was at a Husker Du gig where I was later sick next to one of the infamous pillars, barely noticed by punters and staff.

Sarah Hall

The Riverside pictured in Newcastle University's Courier, 1985, and right, an advert from 1987.

I started going to the Riverside at 14. Kylie's *I Should Be So Lucky* was in the charts then and I was determined I would never hear it as I hated that sort of music, leaping up to turn the TV off if it came on. I'd managed never to have to sit through the entire song. Being all post-modern and ironic, when the Riverside bar had to close at 11pm (though the club could stay open until 1am) to get people to stop dancing and go and get last orders they'd put Kylie on and THAT was the first time I heard Kylie … at the Riverside! I got the irony of it. Everyone would rush to the bar and get about 87 pints. That's probably why the carpet was such an awful mess and a health hazard. Everyone was very young … seemingly about 14 … nobody had their real age on their membership card. I saw New Model Army on their fifth anniversary there, the day after I finished my last GCSE exam in 1989. That was so good!

Kemi Kilburn

I got a job in the Jubilee pub when I was 17. It was Newcastle's main rock bar and I loved every minute. The City Tavern and the Hotspur were other favourites. Susie's upstairs was a bikers' bar. We hung out at the top end of town while the trendy people who went to Julie's would be at the bottom end of town. The two groups didn't mix. It was a foreign country.

There was a rock crowd and a trendy crowd, and a wacky alternative crowd, which was bit punk. You drank in different pubs. The Broken Doll was punk and alternative. There was Rockshots, the Bier Keller and the Dog and Parrot where I also worked. I was in the rock crowd, though had links with others.

Nicola Booth

Some of the rock crowd rock at the Jubilee, September 1983.

The Julie's bus was an open top double-decker that ran in the summer. It would pick people up from pubs and take them to Julie's. It was all disco in the early 1980s, then soul. In complete contrast, the Mayfair was all rock, and was amazing on a Friday and Saturday night. It was licensed until 2am and everyone tried to get in before 10pm when it was free. It was the best rock club in the country. People came from Nottingham, Leeds and London. The best band I ever saw there was AC/DC with Bon Scott – sadly that was his last ever performance. I told my mum I was going to the youth club and when I got in at 2am there was a policeman sitting with my mum. He said he'd leave us to it! I was grounded for months.

Nicola Booth

TIFFANY'S Newcastle
HEAVY ROCK SPECIAL
on
Wednesday, 21st July, 1982
we present
2 SUPER GROUPS
Hellenbach
and
Emerson
plus HEAVY DISCO
8 p.m. to 1 a.m.

Admission with this leaflet or
a Tiffany's privilege pass **ONLY £1**

Don't forget Tiffany's Rock Scene
8 p.m. to 1 a.m. each Monday

John Wm. Dowling & Son, 3 Charlotte Sq., Newcastle

One night club that I really enjoyed was the Junction. This was actually in the Hustler pool club on Northumberland Street, much more my type of thing, especially since if you arrived early enough there was a free buffet, which was mainly chips – cold if you got there too late!

Wednesday night, if I remember rightly, was Grand Central. This was held in a room in Tuxedo Junction. The DJ would play just about whatever music we asked him to, as long as we promised to get up and dance. I think we were kidding ourselves, but we used to call ourselves the floor show – we were proper poseurs. It did seem to get everyone else up dancing, though, 'everyone' being mainly nurses on a night out. We were in our element.

Paul and friends at Grand Central – the floor show.

Other favourite places were the Burton, the Trent House, the Barley Mow and the Baltic. The last two were on the Quayside. I did occasionally go to Madison's, Julie's and Reflexions, but these clubs were all much more mainstream, playing whatever was in the top ten; not really my scene. Other places I sometimes went were Balmbras in the Bigg Market, the Half Moon and the Beehive.

In the early eighties if you walked through Shieldfield, Jesmond or Heaton, there seemed to be a party on every corner. If I was walking back to my flat on Osborne Road in Jesmond, I would make sure I had a couple of cans on me and if I heard music coming from a flat or a house, I would knock on the door, say I was a friend of Billy's, then bang! I was in. My girlfriend Jenny used to tell me off, saying I would be found dead in a dustbin in a back lane one day.

Paul Merrit

In the early 80s Newcastle had, as far as I can remember, five record shops: Callers, Windows, Volume, Virgin and HMV. All the record shop workers met and drank in the Haymarket pub, (all except the staff from HMV, though no one ever found out why). It used to get seriously crowded.

The girls always 'went' in pairs or groups and packed their handbags with toilet roll before going into the bar. Not that it was a dangerous bar, we just enjoyed a proper natter away from the men folk and their constant talk of music.

The Haymarket, 1987, shortly before demolition.

What was definitely the world's worst chip shop was only a few doors down from this bar. You had to have had more than a couple of pints to even consider stepping inside!

Chris and Annie Moir

After hours

I seemed to spend a lot of the eighties engaged in the task of finding a drink at a civilized hour; no easy thing when pubs closed at 10.30pm and Newcastle's strict licensing laws meant there were only a handful of radgie nightclubs. But by some happy quirk in the legislation, drink *could* be had after hours if it accompanied a meal. I never fancied food after a session in a pub – kebabs excepted – but there were a few places keen to exploit this loophole and give people what they really wanted.

In 1982, my old boss Derek Kirkup from Fynd opened a restaurant called the Barn, in a courtyard off Leazes Road that was completely hidden from passers-by. The tone for his new establishment was set on the opening night, when a guest allegedly tipped something narcotic into the punch, causing one or two people to run around the place buck-naked. I played (fully clad) in the band that night and our guitarist fell asleep on top of a Calor Gas heater, but despite several years of painful skin grafts he still says it was the best party he's ever been to.

Derek was a charismatic and well-connected man so you might be jostling at the bar with skint local artists, Shakespearian actors from the Theatre Royal, or some landed gentry, while he held court till seven or eight in the morning. Food was available if you wanted it, and to be fair, some people did treat the place as a restaurant. But most used the Barn as a late-night or early morning watering hole, where you'd be guaranteed some interesting company. Derek Kirkup died in 1986, a huge loss to the city.

The Barn made an effort to look and act like a restaurant, unlike Shaun Wilson and Ray Callan's venture at the North Eastern Hotel. They hired a large function room in the premises on Carliol Square in 1982, where they ran their Packet of Cornflakes 'alternative disco', pulling in several hundred thirsty but not especially hungry punters every Saturday night. We paid a couple of quid to get in and were each issued with a cold meat pie, which was immediately discarded and trodden into the floor as people got down to the serious business of drinking and dancing. After a few months the police raided the place and closed it down, declaring that a pie wasn't a substantial meal.

Brothers Mike and Pete Gosney were next to chance their luck, opening the Jewish Mother restaurant in an old synagogue on Leazes Lane. This undoubtedly started out as a serious venture, with a proper menu and live music. But the Gosneys were having way too much fun to worry about the catering when the bar was doing so well, and didn't seem to mind that people treated the place as a club rather than a restaurant. Unfortunately the police did mind, and when a coach-load arrived in plain clothes and weren't offered a meal with their drinks, the game was up and the place closed down.

The Jewish Mother might start to quieten down around three or four in the morning, then we'd head off to Josephine's where things

would be just starting to liven up. Keith Crombie was a good friend of Derek Kirkup and made it his mission to keep his and the Barn's spirit alive. He rented a four-storey townhouse on an alleyway off Pink Lane, a building that later became part of the Forth Hotel. As chance would have it, the previous owner had decked the ground floor out as a restaurant, and although Keith believed this is what Josephine's was, I never saw any food there.

You had to use a 'special knock', then you'd hear a rattle of chains and the door would crack open a few inches, and a bearded face would appear in the gap. If you were his sort of person – or any female – you were admitted to a comically small room with a bar, tables and a dancefloor. Keith catered for the night time economy, providing the likes of bar workers, bouncers and burglars with somewhere to unwind when their work was completed. I was fascinated by the mix of off-duty coppers, criminals and their barristers, gangsters, and characters from Keith's Club a'GoGo and Downbeat days; and the respect they had for him, as he moved among them in a full admiral's uniform.

It was always broad daylight when I left Josephine's. But I'd have been ejected earlier were I there the night it was raided by the police, a couple of dozen of whom climbed in through a back window. There was a court case, in which it was legally deemed that Keith was 'not a fit and proper person', something with which he heartily agreed. He proved this by opening the Rendezvous Jazz Café a few yards away in 1989, and the fun continued into another decade.

Marshall Hall

Top, the legendary Keith Crosbie at Josephine's.

Above, on 14 July 1989 a group of West Jesmond Juniors commemorated Bastille Day, by marching aristocrats to the Rendezvous Café, where, according to the Crack magazine, there was a minor riot.

The silver screen

I was a huge Tom Cruise fan and we saw all the classics like *Top Gun* and *Cocktail* in the Odeon or the ABC. Smokers sat on one side of the audience and non-smokers sat on the other. What was the point? We all came out smelling of cigarette smoke. And it was worse if you had friends who were smokers – because you had to sit on that side with them. I choked my way through many a film, burying my nose into my scarf and trying not to complain.

Kirsty Ferry

I t was cheaper for me to buy a ticket for the all night film show at the ABC on a Friday (mostly a horror theme) and have a kip there on the plush seats than to get a taxi back home to Ryton. Some came dressed for the horror nights in appropriate costumes. It was a real miss after it closed!

Marshall Hall

The Haymarket ABC cinema, Percy Street, in 1984 soon after closure.

69

I went to see *The Empire Strikes Back* as part of a double bill at the Odeon in 1980 … we had to queue round the back. It ran for a staggering 14 weeks. There was a scary cartoon *Chico the Rainmaker*, which they used to show before the main feature at kids' club films on a Saturday. Utterly terrifying! And we saw *Flash Gordon*, featuring Peter Duncan from Blue Peter before he got killed off.

Kemi Kilburn

11 August 1989 and the queue for Batman at the Cannon on Westgate Road snakes round the block.

Gosforth's Royalty Cinema in 1984. Suburban cinemas didn't do well in the 1980s. In 1980 the Royalty was bought by Paul Burton who managed Dexys Midnight Runners. There were occasional concerts but magistrates refused it a full license. Film audiences were disappointing and the cinema finally closed at the end of 1981.

The Tyneside Cinema, January 1983. Inset, the circle, 1989.

The Tyneside was where we mostly went if we had a babysitter and we saw lots of European films there. The annual Film Festival was always interesting. We could also go to the Odeon, the Haymarket ABC before it closed, and the Cannon on Westgate Road, and to the Jesmond Picture House occasionally. When the kids got older we took them to the cinema too. It was an important treat in the school holidays. I fell asleep in The Gobots film at the Odeon in charge of a party of small boys in 1985. (Anna Flowers)

Beauty and the Swamp Monster at the Tyneside Summer Exhibition

This story concerns the Miss Evening Chronicle competition, which took place at the 1983 Tyneside Summer Exhibition. My sister, Rachel was taking part, so Mum had made me promise to be there to support her. Me, my girlfriend Jenny, and my best friend John turned up at the entrance about half an hour before the competition was due to start, and as we got to the gate, I realised with horror that even if we put all our money together, we still only had enough to pay one of us in.

For those of you who are not old enough or who have forgotten about the Tyneside Summer Exhibition, businesses or brands would have promotion tents advertising their products, and there would be a few fairground rides, dodgem cars, waltzers etc. Security was very tight. A high fence ran from one end of the Exhibition Park lake, all the way round the perimeter of the exhibition, to the other end of the lake. Security guards patrolled, making it very hard to sneak in. Even so, I suggested to John and Jenny that if we put all our money together we would be able to pay Jenny in and then John and I would find a way of sneaking in.

I knew that climbing the fence was out of the question, as it was too high and there were too many people watching so I suggested that once Jenny was safely in, John and I would sit on the side of the lake, then slide in, swim quietly over to the exhibition side and climb out. I knew that once we got past half way it would be very difficult for them to prove that we had not got in from the exhibition side. We waited until we saw Jenny, easy to spot in a lovely pink 50s dress with her hair up in a bee-hive style, standing waiting for us to make our move.

On that cue we both slid into the water. The first shock I got was how cold it was. The second shock was that although I had always thought the lake was at least six foot deep (it was murky so you could not see the bottom) it was actually only came up to my hips. We knew we would be spotted if we just plodged across, so we decided to slide down onto our bellies and push ourselves along the bottom with our hands and feet. Almost immediately I felt a sharp pain at the front of my left thigh but not knowing what it was, I just pushed on. Jenny gazed at us both as if we were completely mad! Once we got past the half way point I said, 'Right John. If we're stopped, remember to tell them we got in from the exhibition side and forgot to keep our tickets.' What I found scary was that once or twice I nearly stuck to the very slimy bottom. When we eventually got to the exhibition side, we pulled ourselves out, unbelievably without attracting any attention. We both stood up, to be met by Jenny, who said in horror, 'My God! Look at you both. You look like a couple of swamp monsters.'

We looked at each other and indeed we were covered, head to toe in green slime, bits of duckweed,

Camel rides, just one of the attractions at Tyneside Summer Exhibition, 1983.

and, as Jenny quickly pointed out, a horrendous smell. I soon found out why I had felt a pain in my thigh as I had a nasty cut and a rip in my trousers. I pointed out to John that it would have been better if we had simply dug a tunnel. 'Anyway' I said, 'come on. The competition will be starting.'

We eventually found a large tent, with a sign saying *Evening Chronicle* and as we went in, people near us parted like the Red Sea. We stood at the back, people nearby screwing up their noses at the awful smell. One by one each contestant came on to the stage to be met by the compère, Mr David Macbeth Senior (who was, I was told, the owner of Grey's Casino), each girl in turn telling him how they wanted to help the world's starving children and go shark fishing etc. Eventually my sister Rachel had her turn, looking absolutely beautiful. The only girl I knew who actually looked better was my girlfriend, Jenny, but I suppose I would say that, wouldn't I? 'No family resemblance there then,' John said to me. I had to agree with him.

You can imagine our joy when Mr Macbeth Senior proclaimed 'And the winner, and the new Miss Evening Chronicle is Miss Rachel Merrit, from Gosforth'. I could see my mum, dad and grandma jumping for joy at the front. Rachel, I thought, controlled herself very well. She glanced to the back of the hall and we made eye contact. I put both thumbs up and mouthed the words, 'Well done!' Even under the circumstances Rachel, with a look of mock horror, mouthed what I thought to be the words 'What the hell happened to you?' Mum began to look around for me, then fought her way through the audience followed by a couple of important-looking ladies, who I assumed to be modelling people that Rachel knew. When she got to me, as she started to say 'This is my son, Paul' the proud look on her face turned to one of horror.

'Oh Mum, me and John fell in the lake'

'But Paul, you're twenty years old! When will you stop doing these ridiculous things?'

'I don't think he ever will, Norma,' Jenny replied.

Paul Merrit

A proud Rachel Merrit, centre, wins the Evening Chronicle beauty competition, 1983, and inset, brother Paul, in clean jeans, early 1980s

The last Tyneside Summer Exhibition

On 29 July 1987 I went with Mam and Dad and nephew Mark, age five, to the Tyneside Summer Exhibition. Admission charges were £1.80 for adults and 90p concessions although if you were unemployed or on long term sick you had to show proof of benefits to qualify for the concession. The family ticket was great value at £4.50 to admit two adults and three children, no proof of ownership required! There were attractions for everyone including the Red Devils, a high wire act, hot air balloons, bands, clowns, trade/arts and crafts stalls, flower and agricultural shows and cookery demonstrations. The highlight of my nephew's day was being able to climb over and inside a Chieftain tank.

The weather remained fair for most of the week and attendance was up on the previous year. Despite the success of the show the *Evening Chronicle* reported on 17 February 1988 'Top Tyneside Show scrapped' due to falling attendances and a cash crisis. After 25 years a great Tyneside attraction was lost.

Hazel Nixon

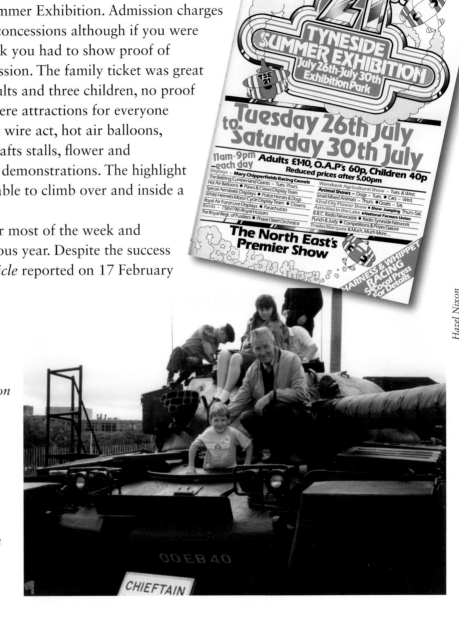

Hazel Nixon

Top, an advertisement from North East Times, summer 1983.

Right, Dad and nephew Mark on a Chieftain tank at the Tyneside Summer Exhibition 29 July 1987.

PUMP UP THE VOLUME

M|A|R|R|S, 1987

The best audience in the world

I started as City Hall manager in early 1981 and my first gig was Ian Gillen and Deep Purple, but the best gig I ran at City Hall, the best one ever, happened just a couple of months later on 11 May 1981 – Bruce Springsteen and the E Street Band. Around 3,000 people tell me they were at that concert, which is funny as the building only seats 2,000!

Lindisfarne's Christmas concerts in the early 80s were something everyone at City Hall looked forward to and dreaded at the same time as they came at the end of a busy season. All the stewards would moan about ten nights of Lindisfarne, but by the end of the first night there they would be at the back, dancing along to the music. They enjoyed it as much as anyone when we got there. They were great nights.

Before there were any other big venues, City Hall was the only place to accommodate a big audience. Motorhead performed for three and four nights, Dire Straits did four nights. Elton John started a world tour here in 1983 as we were well known for our great audiences, and our reputation was second to none. Everyone wanted to play here. We had Eric Clapton, Phil Collins and all the massive acts. It's not the building – the stage isn't big enough, we don't have enough dressing rooms or facilities, but the audiences keep bringing the artists back. If I could bottle the atmosphere I could make a fortune.

Meatloaf's production manager asked his wife where she wanted to come and see him when they toured Europe – and she said Newcastle. She'd seen all the kids at Malibu Beach with their European tour t-shirts listing London, Madrid, Paris, Berlin … and Newcastle, and so it must be the place to go. She wondered if we were the size of Madison Square Gardens. Of course when they got here and

City Hall, Newcastle-upon-Tyne

Philips Compact Disc by arrangement with
Outlaw present—
DIRE STRAITS Live in '85
Show Starts 8.00 prompt No Support & No Interval
Wednesday, 4th December 1985
Evening 8.00
BALCONY
£8.50
L   17

A.B. Cooper (Printers) Ltd., Chorlton, Manchester

Retain this portion

No Tickets Exchanged nor Money Refunded
No Cameras or Recording Equipment
Official Programmes sold only in the Theatre

LINDISFARNE CHRISTMAS SHOWS
10 GREAT YEARS
Christmas 1976 to Christmas 1985

Lindisfarne
**CHRISTMAS
SHOW '85**
NOW BOOKING
FOR
7 DAYS ONLY

LINDISFARNE AT THE CITY HALL
10th ANNIVERSARY
December 1976 to December 1985

CITY HALL, Newcastle-upon-Tyne

Metro Radio in Assn. with Barry McKay presents—

Lindisfarne
The Concert

LINDISFARNE CHRISTMAS SHOWS 1976–1982
Thursday, 30th December 1982 at 7.30

BALCONY
£4.00

J 14

A. B. Cooper (Printers) Ltd., Manchester

Tickets cannot be exchanged nor money refunded under any circumstances except for cancellation of the show. Retain this portion.

METRO RADIO

Lindisfarne started the 1980s performing nine Newcastle City Hall Christmas shows in a row and by 1984 the event had grown to 12 nights, playing to 27,600 people (including 200 fans seated each night on the stage behind the band), not much below the capacity of St James Park at the time. There was no annual show anywhere in the UK to compare to what happened at the City Hall every Christmas. (Barry McKay)

she saw the hall was only the size of Meatloaf's lounge she wondered why is he playing here? Meatloaf said, 'stand in the audience and you'll know why'… After the show, hair all over, wet through, she said she'd been all round the world but she'd never ever seen an audience get or give as much energy before. The same artists still come back … they're a bit more staid now.

Were there any difficult artists? The Stranglers in 1983 or 1984 tried to get me to take all the security out of the front of the hall as they didn't want any to be visible. I said, no as it's there to protect the hall, not you. There was a big row! I stuck my ground and it was ok. A few days later they played Hammersmith Odeon, with no security, and around £5000 worth of damage was done to the seating.

Bucks Fizz played on 11 December 1986 and that concert resulted in disaster for the group. After the gig they left in a coach to go the Gosforth Park Hotel. There were road works on the Great North Road and a lorry came the wrong way down the coned area, smashing into the bus head-on, injuring all the members of the group, particularly Mike Nolan, who suffered severe head injuries. It could have been even more tragic as I was in the car just in front with my daughter, who was about seven or eight, but I got through the lights at the Haymarket and went ahead. My daughter was in the back of my car, and she would have been killed if we had been caught at the lights too.

Most people have been really pleasant. We didn't

interfere; we let them get on with the job and the show. Make a happy audience and you have a happy City Hall manager.

There are always people who try to blag their way in but it was never really a problem as there aren't all that many doors to get into the City Hall. It was more a problem of getting people out, because of going down to the front, getting drunk, trying to get on stage, or over the balcony.

The 1980s was also the time of Mrs Brown, a very strange old lady, who just used to walk in; she never paid for a ticket. It was a weird situation that went on for years. Everyone knew she was there and that she hadn't paid, but she was a little old lady into heavy metal! The fans knew all about her and Status Quo dedicated a song to her. She'd just find a seat (and there always was a spare seat as nobody stayed sitting down). I asked Mrs Brown why she liked heavy metal one night and she said 'well I'm deaf and it's the only music I can hear'. I was told that one night on the Metro she was being bothered by some punks or suchlike and three or four heavy metal fans also on the train stepped in to protect her. We had to stop her coming in the end. The final straw was her bringing in some fish and chips, which she'd got out of a bin on Northumberland Road. She didn't come back after that. What happened to Mrs Brown?

Peter Brennan

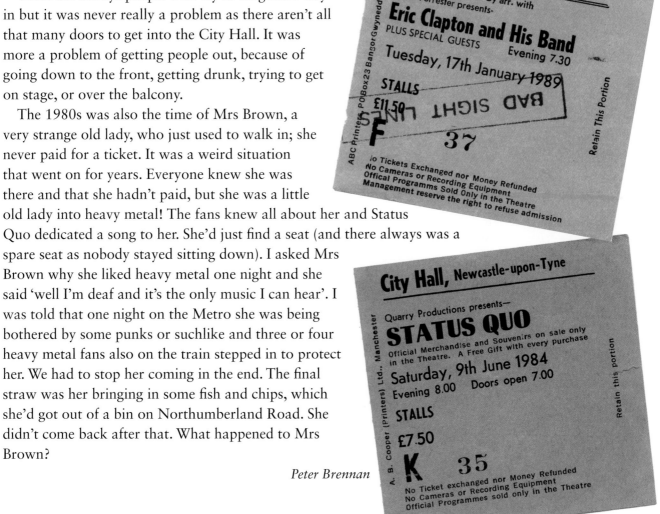

The best place for music in Newcastle was the City Hall. I saw Thin Lizzy, the Scorpions, UFO, Motorhead, and Ozzy Osbourne. Some of the rock crowd became roadies so we got backstage passes if we blagged enough. People would sleep out all night to get tickets. I slept out a couple of times from about 10 at night. I'd get my ticket at nine in the morning and hop on the bus to school with my uniform in my bag. My friend and I would say we were sleeping at each other's houses. We were never found out. Rush tickets went on sale one January and an ambulance had to be called in the early morning as it had been so cold that a guy's feet had frozen to the inside of his sleeping bag. It was proper rock and roll.

You'd go in with your ticket, go upstairs to the toilet and wrap your ticket round a stone and throw it down from the window to your friend outside … who'd come in with it, then do it again. Everyone my age will tell you the same story.

The bands would come out of the stage door and chat. It's not the same now.

Nicola Booth

CITY HALL
Northumberland Road, Newcastle upon Tyne
—
Sunday, 18th May, 1980, at 7.30 p.m.
—
STRAIGHT MUSIC
presents
BLACK SABBATH

AREA £4.50 SEAT
75p
Booking Agents: City Hall Box Office
Northumberland Road, Newcastle upon Tyne (Tel 20007)

SMITH PRINT GROUP

Photos and ticket Nicola Booth

Nicola met many stars backstage at the City Hall. Above left, Iron Maiden's Bruce Dickinson, May 1983, and right, with Phil Lynot in 1983.

The early 80s saw the steady demise of some of the greatest bands of the glam rock era. The City Hall hosted the Sweet in 1981 and the three remaining members (without lead singer Brian Connolly) did their best to entertain an audience that just filled the first three rows. I did meet the band after the show though, and so did everyone else who was at the gig! Slade performed there in December 1981 and although there was still as much excitement and enthusiasm when they played a certain Christmas song it was evident from the 'greatest hits' that the show centred around that there wasn't much more they could offer.

The bigger names however were still doing alright. Ritchie Blackmore's Rainbow still had their regular cult following in 1981 as did The Who in the same year. Both gigs sold out as soon as tickets became available and both groups performed classic sets.

Ozzy Osbourne was still going strong following his revival with The Blizzard of Oz as were his previous band, Black Sabbath. Deep Purple frontmen Ian Gillan and David Coverdale always had time to stop off in Newcastle with their respective bands whenever they were touring. And of course it goes without saying that Lindisfarne, fresh from their reformation in 1978 continued with their traditional Christmas Concerts. On each of these occasions it meant dipping into the 'concert fund'.

Nicola Booth

Simon Carey   *Nicola Booth meets Ozzy Osbourne at Newcastle's Virgin Records, Eldon Square, in 1982.*

Jimmy Page, 23 November 1988

It was a typically cold autumnal Newcastle night when my friend Mark and I made the journey from Sunderland (where we were students) to the 'Toon'. Mark was more of a 'metaller' than me, I was strictly John Peel and indie but I'd loved Led Zeppelin since I was 12. It's a right of passage thing – mate's elder brother lends you *Zep 4* and *Presence* and then you're hooked.

We queued up outside amidst a sea of denim and leather jackets sporting patches for UFO/Rainbow/AC/DC/Sabbath et al, big Brian May poodle perms and ultra tight stonewashed jeans. Not 80s fashions victims, just your average metal crowd. Really neither of us had high hopes that night. How wrong we were. We had good seats in the balcony to the right of the stage, there was much beery good humour from the Geordies around us and Page played a belter mix of tunes, all impeccably performed. That night was special, a rarity. Seeing Jimmy Page live was one I could always use to out-trump someone in the 'which bands have you seen?' stakes.

We probably had a lecture to attend the following morning but somehow it didn't matter, we'd just seen a bona fide guitar hero in a cracking venue with a cracking crowd!

Richard Higgins

The Boss's best gig

Aged 15 in 1981, I had a total obsession with music and going to gigs. From my first gig experience at the age of 13 in 1978, that was it – nothing else was as important in my life. Of course money was limited, but my best pal was loosely related to one of the doormen at the City Hall so we often just turned up ticketless to a gig looking a bit sweet and pathetic and he would let us sneak in and watch from the back. We saw hundreds of shows in the 80s.

This particular gig was a bit different – I was in town in the late afternoon and thought I would walk past the hall to catch a bit of the buzz surrounding this international superstar. Of course, to the general public of Newcastle (and indeed the UK) Bruce was yet to become the household name that *Born In The USA* would make him, but I hung around the fringes of a very in-the-know music crowd who had educated me way beyond my years regarding the international music scene, and I knew just how cool Bruce was. As I walked past the stage door I stopped to talk to one of the local crew who I was friendly with, and during that short chat an American crew guy walked up to me and handed me a ticket for the gig. He just said 'Here use this, it's gonna be a great show hun', and walked off. I looked at this ticket, saw it was front row balcony, walked around the front to the old box office, and asked one of the women there if it was genuine. She confirmed it was, and just said 'Eeh, you lucky thing pet.'

So later that evening I wandered in alone to the City Hall to one of the best gigs of my life. My strongest memories are my horror when I thought everyone was booing him, which turned to relief when it sunk in that the noise around me was not the sound of 'BOOOOOOOO!' but 'BRROOOOOOCE!'; the sweat almost dripping off the walls; the sight of EVERYONE around me dancing. Bruce with that guitar slung so low, swaggering across the stage and then sliding on his knees to the feet of big Clarence Clemmons who looked like he had never had so much fun in his whole life. I staggered out of the door at the end of that evening with an exhausted, euphoric crowd to get a lift home from my ever-patient Dad (the gig had gone on way past curfew) and go into school the next day, completely unable

Bill Norman

The Boss and Clarence Clemmons on stage, City Hall, 11 May 1981.

to convey to any of my pals exactly what I had witnessed. Something of pure magic.

As a therapist who is often hired for artist massage, I was thrilled to be booked to do a pre-show massage for Bruce when he played at Sunderland's Stadium of Light in 2012. To my delight he was incredibly friendly and chatty, and when he asked me where I was from and I told him his immediate response was 'Newcastle! Home of The Animals!' followed by 'Man, I did an amazing gig at the City Hall there once.' When I told him I had been in the crowd, he lifted me off the ground with a hug and said 'You guys gave me a memory that keeps me in this game – magic like that … wow!'

Carolyn Shearer

Bruce was well known, but not the muscle-bound thug rock superstar of *Born in the USA* three years later. Indeed he was still the wiry kid with something to prove in many ways. His fifth album, *The River*, had come out some six months earlier to rave reviews. Most Brucophiles reckoned it would have made a stunning single album with quite a bit of filler but hell we would have accepted him singing Phil Collins songs at that point in time.

This was the first proper tour in the UK since the disastrous 'Finally the world is ready for Bruce Springsteen' at the Hammy Odeon in 1975 and, if memory serves, Newcastle was the opening gig. Originally scheduled for 31 March it was rescheduled through illness for 11 May which, as it turned out, was significant for music in another way being the day Bob Marley died.

I thought 'palpable sense of expectation' was just a phrase used by rock journalists when they ran out of inspiration. It wasn't that night – you really could feel magic in the air as I entered the City Hall with a couple of friends.

But you know, the other main star that night was the City Hall itself – simply perfect. Magnificent acoustics and an audience who knew how to rock, sing and shout BROOOOOOCE!

Bill Norman

CITY HALL, Newcastle-upon-Tyne

Harvey Goldsmith Ent. presents—

BRUCE SPRINGSTEEN & THE E STREET BAND

IN CONCERT

Tuesday, 31st March 1981
Evening 7-30

BALCONY

F

£4.50

11

Retain this portion

A. B. Cooper (Printers) Ltd., MANCHESTER

Bill Norman

84

The City Hall audience embraces Bruce Springsteen on 11 May, 1981. Unforgettable!

Rocking at St James Park

I worked on most of the big stadium concerts ... Bob Dylan, Springsteen, the Stones and so on. St James Park held about 30-40,000. It was fun, a busman's holiday for me.

The Stones was the first in 1982. On their rider they said they wanted an enclosure for their dressing rooms at what was then the back of the Leazes End. They wanted a garden in the middle of it with a fish pond! I remember we got someone from Hexham to come in and provide all this, with fish, and a little stream, grass, and so on. It cost an absolute fortune and they never saw it because they came in by coach, went straight on stage, came off stage, got back in the coach and away, with a police escort. It got taken up the next day and back to Hexham. It was rock and roll!

Peter Brennan (City Hall Manager)

The very first time I filmed for *The Tube* was the Stones at St James Park in 1982. The Stones pulled up in a car and Jagger jumped out and danced around in a circle with Graham the cameraman. We'd never seen a cameraman dancing with the Stones before.

Jeff Brown (Tube Associate Producer)

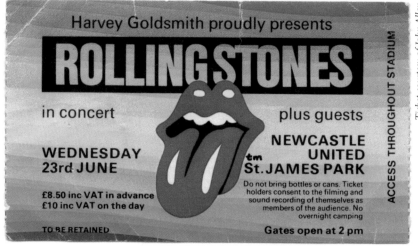

Ticket courtesy of John Allan

From A Cartoonist's Chronicle, Geoff Laws

I drew caricatures for the Chronicle. For inspiration I'd open the window by my desk at Thomson House to listen to the bands rehearse before the concert. (Geoff Laws)

When the Rolling Stones played at St James Park, it was a huge spectacle with a stage set that was revolutionary at the time and a fireworks display at the end. It was a hot summer's day and the ground had open access so you could wander around to get the best vantage point. The support acts, J Geils Band and George Thorogood and the Destroyers got everyone rocking before a tumultuous reception when the Stones swaggered on stage. It wasn't the best sound system but they played for two and a half hours and had 50,000 people jumping.

After the gig we went to the Broken Doll. The rear of the bar had ready pulled pints of ale in anticipation of the arrival of thirsty rock fans. They were not wrong as no alcohol was allowed in St James Park. The jukebox was blasting out Stones songs. I still treasure a Broken Doll t-shirt that I won on the day. And the ticket price? £8.50!!!!

Chris Mason

At St James Park we saw Bob Dylan, looking like a small pixie holding the crowd enthralled. The experience was messianic! We missed Springsteen's marvellous show, but friends drove all the way from Ullapool and back to see him.

Guy Hall

Lindisfarne was THE group of the time. I went to a concert at St James Park to see Lindisfarne. The support act was some bloke in a flowery shirt, called Santana, then this other bloke came on and sort of growled for a bit, so we left early. The growler was called Bob Dylan. We found out afterwards that he was famous. But I swear the advertising hoardings had Lindisfarne in bigger letters! After the first year, when we lived in rented houses, we stayed for the annual Christmas Lindisfarne concert at Newcastle City Hall. There was nothing like it! Everyone was standing on the seats by the end of the first song. It was THE Christmas feeling.

Julia Norman

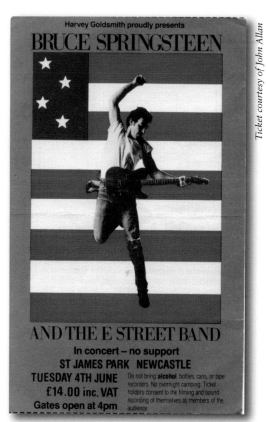

Harvey Goldsmith proudly presents
BRUCE SPRINGSTEEN
AND THE E STREET BAND
In concert – no support
ST JAMES PARK NEWCASTLE
TUESDAY 4TH JUNE
£14.00 inc. VAT
Do not bring **alcohol**, bottles, cans, or tape recorders. No overnight camping. Ticket holders consent to the filming and sound recording of themselves as members of the audience.
Gates open at 4pm

Ticket courtesy of John Allan

On 5 July 1984 I went to see Bob Dylan at St James Park. Local lads Lindsfarne were first on the bill and as the afternoon wore on I kept my place waiting for Santana to come on. They played a blistering set of Latin beats including *Oye Como Va*. I kept my place near the front hoping to snap a few pictures. Dylan came on ably supported by Mick Taylor formerly of the Stones. He only really reacted to the crowd when they started singing to *It Ain't me Babe* on acoustic guitar and harmonica, a smile creeping across his face. He played his hits but was even better when he accompanied himself with guitar and harmonica.

Juan Fitzgerald

The 1980s passed in a blur of small children, sleepless nights, trying days at work and not enough money to cover the bills at the end of each month. Open-air concerts in Newcastle seemed like a bad idea – it was bound to rain, even in July, and there was no way we could get to St James Park when the gates opened at 2pm. So with kids settled with a babysitter we decided to walk down to listen to Dylan outside in Strawberry Place. It was a perfect evening, warm and clear. Santana were on stage. There can't have been more than six of us outside, the stewards were looking bored; they waved us over. Thinking they wanted a chat, to our amazement we were ushered in! As we made our way down onto the rear of the covered pitch, Dylan was just starting what was to be a memorable set. Newcastle followed concerts in Nantes, Paris and Grenoble, and Dylan clearly had yet to come to terms with an uninspired rhythm section and a wayward lead guitarist, Mick Taylor, though I remember a particularly fine *Masters of War*. Dylan commented 'I think that this song still has some relevance today'. Playing in front of an English-speaking crowd seemed to lift Dylan and the atmosphere became almost palpable, as he reinvented many of his classic songs. The sound of 30,000 singing along with Dylan and his acoustic guitar to *Girl from the North Country* is still very special. The bootleggers were quick to satisfy demand and within a week we had bought from the quayside a double cassette tape, *Dylan at the Park* so we could relive the time when we saw Dylan for free.

Anthony Flowers

The crowd wait in the sun on 5 July 1984. Some might have been waiting for Santana, many might have been waiting for Lindisfarne, but most were waiting for Bob himself.

Harvey Goldsmith & Mel Bush by arrangement with
Bill Graham proudly present

BOB DYLAN
SANTANA
in concert

NEWCASTLE UNITED
St. James Park

Do not bring bottles or cans. Ticket holders consent to the filming and sound recording of themselves as members of the audience. No overnight camping.

**THURSDAY
5TH JULY 1984**

£11 inc VAT in advance
£12 inc VAT on the day

Gates open 2.00 p.m.

TO BE RETAINED

Proper post-punks

I was a big fan of Orange Juice from Glasgow's Postcard label, and I made a t-shirt with dolphins on – it's from an album cover. They weren't very big at the time.

After the Bier Keller on Waterloo Street there came Dingwalls. It was downstairs. We went from *The Tube* on to Dingwalls for gigs … it was a natural progression. I bought the singer from Orange Juice, Edwyn Collins, a checky shirt, and he wore my shirt on the stage that night! My heart melted. The guitarist's wife and I became penpals and I went to stay with them in Scotland. Sometimes they didn't let us in at Dingwalls as we were too young … so we waited outside to get autographs.

Tracey and I did the whole spiky hair thing. I had mine cut like Terry Hall when he was in Fun Boy Three.

Our favourite bar was the Broken Doll. We hung around the Handyside Arcade too. We were proper punks, or so we thought! It was a lovely combination of hippy and punk there … joss sticks, tartan trousers, mohicans. We'd go to the Kard Bar for posters and badges.

I was a big Hazel O'Connor fan and where I lived in Low Fell the local cinema cost £1. I was obsessed with *Breaking Glass* and I went every day during the week that it was on. Mam caught me trying to steal coins from our phone money box to pay for tickets and there were tears. We bought music from Volume Records on Ridley place next to the baked potato shop. I couldn't afford a potato but Tracey could.

Paula Ginger

Looking back to an earlier time, Teddy Boys in their best drapes on Waterloo Street on their way to rock at the Hoffbrauhaus in 1982. The Bier Keller is on the left, along with Scamps, Rockshots and Studio 1-2-3-4.

The birth of Kitchenware Records

It's 1982, I am working as manager of the HMV record shop in Newcastle. At 19, the youngest and possibly most reckless manager; alongside me, Phil Mitchell, equally reckless and an encyclopedia of soul.

I get BORED rigid with the local music scene and the current music du jour, New Romantic. This wasn't supposed to happen after Punk Rock and Disco ruled our formative years! An idea! Let's start a club. Let's get everyone with a spark together and START SOMETHING!

I rally a group of like minded people – friends like Paul Ludford and Phil and we open a club, The Soul Kitchen. It's a once in a blue moon club that brings acts like Fire Engines!, Aztec Camera, A Certain Ratio – bands we actually want to see – innovators – to Newcastle. The Soul Kitchen expands – Jenny Barrett makes Kitch-In-Wear clothes, Matt Hyphen and Paula Goldberg form East Orange and provide ART. The Soul Kitchen attracts NEW! Unusual! Hungry!

We persuade New Order to play our club thanks to Rob Gretton of Factory records and now we have the money to make records. Kitchenware Records is born!

Now I didn't have a clue how to make records but I knew that Hurrah! The Daintees, Prefab Sprout and The Kane Gang should all be making them so … we worked on instinct – hired studios – self produced – found the means of production and Bang! Newcastle's first true independent record label was born.

It was pure conceit that enabled us to convince Chris Cowey to let us make a documentary about

Keith Armstrong, founder of Soul Kitchen and Kitchenware Records.

US on Tyne Tees and then convince the trailblazing Malcolm Gerrie to give Kitchenware its own spot on *The Tube*.

We were game changers, they were game changers and at the HEART of everything, a love for our beloved home NEWCASTLE! Tell the world, it's where it's at!

Now, since its 80s birth, Kitchenware has been involved in bringing some of the most memorable and successful music from Newcastle to the world. We were lucky then. It was a time of strikes, riots, and Thatcher but it was also a time of *Viz Comic*, the Trent House Soul explosion and of course, the Soul Kitchen and Kitchenware Records. Out of dirt comes diamonds.

So our slogan – young, gifted and black – referred to the vinyl of our records but also to the true roots of all great popular music.

There follows a guide to our artists in the order they were signed …

Simon McKay

Soul Kitchen happened in clubs such as the Casablanca on the Haymarket, the Bier Keller on Waterloo Street, or alternative nights at Tiffanys.

Hurrah!

Originating as the Green Eyed Children, they took the eye of Jenny Barrett of the Soul Kitchen who recommended them as a support act at the club. We thought GEC was a little too hippy dippy for a young band with such rousing punk/Velvets influence music and suggested they change their name to Hurrah! For Youth which unfortunately, dubiously may have been stolen from a Hitler Youth poster – sorry we hate all fascists but good names are hard to find!

Paul Handyside (vocals, guitar), Taffy Hughes (guitar, vocals, shapes) and Dave Porthouse (bass) shortened the name to Hurrah! and with the first of

Bleddyn Butcher

Looking down on Handyside Arcade, Paul Handyside (right), and Taffy Hughes of Hurrah! 1983.

their many drummers – they got through drummers like Spinal Tap – recorded *The Sun Shines Here*. Not just a record – a clarion call and mission statement for everything Kitchenware would stand for. 'It may be raining where you are, but the Sun Shines Here!' Here, in NEWCASTLE, the greatest place in the world!

The Daintees

So we've booked this studio in London to take Hurrah! down to record their debut single and this skinny bunch of kids, they look like the Bash Street Kids with guitars, are busking outside HMV (where the basement is home to young Kitchenware records). We invite them in, something reminds me of Ry Cooder, the leader, Martin Stephenson, has SOMETHING – that certain divvunt knaa what, as the French might say (if they were Geordies), so there and then we say, get down to London by midnight tonight and we'll record your first single! Luckily, Jamie (guitar) had a working Ford Anglia that the rest of the band could fit into. *Roll On Summertime* was recorded as the second Kitchenware release.

Bleddyn Butcher

Juan Fitzgerald

Martin Stephenson of the Daintees, 1984.
Left, the Daintees at Northumbria University,
photographed by Juan Fitzgerald.

The Kane Gang

Still the only Kitchenware act ever to be signed from a demo tape. What a demo tape! It contained the stone cold soul classic *Brother Brother*. And when we met them – OH BROTHER! Sam and Dave ! Well, Martin (Brammer), Paul (Woods) and Dave(Brewis)! Proper soulboys with great music taste and two front men. Oh yeah that's solid gold dust. Phil Mitchell produced their first single *Brother Brother,* we threw an East Orange Martin Luther King sleeve on it and it was PERFECTION!

Prefab Sprout

Martin McAloon, one man record company and bass player for his brother Paddy's band Prefab Sprout 'don't even think about changing the name' brought *Lions In My Own Garden (Exit Someone)* into HMV one day looking for a stockist. I THOUGHT I'D DIED AND GONE TO HEAVEN!!!

One of the greatest debut singles ever. Made in County Durham by the finest band and written by the BEST songwriter of his generation. So in walk Martin, Paddy, Wendy Smith, Mick Salmon and Feona Attwood. Can we put it out on Kitchenware? Please? We'll lead you to 4 million album sales!

Top, The Kane Gang, 1983.
Right, Paddy McAloon, Prefab Sprout, 1984.

Produced by the Kane Gang's Dave Brewis, we made SWOON – *Songs Written Out Of Necessity*. If we'd never done anything else, ever again, it would have been enough! Prefab Sprout – the last surviving band on the original Kitchenware label. The best ever band to come out of the Great North East. My pleasure.

Keith Armstrong

I bought the Lindisfarne single *Save our Ales* in The Farmer's Rest (they had a few copies behind the bar), which was an Alan Hull protest song about an Aussie Brewery Company trying to take over Newcastle Brewery.

There was a great record shop on Ridley Place called Volume Records where you could get a lot of obscure stuff that wasn't in the charts.

Gary Robinson

VOLUME RECORDS
50,000,000 DELINQUENTS CAN'T BE WRONG

Music fans were rigidly divided into three groups. The club goers, who liked their cover bands and their cheap Federation beer; the rockers who liked their tight trousers, leather jackets and heavy metal; and the eclectic fringe who always wanted to try something new. There were too many narrow minds and pre-conceptions about music. Heavy metal has always had a great following in Newcastle, but the Geordie rock tradition was a ball and chain for many more original acts. Kitchenware Records were a breath of fresh air. They wiped the slate clean and pointed out that bands didn't have to do a residency at the Cooperage then drive to London in a transit van to make the big time. They launched Prefab Sprout and the Kane Gang. Arthur 2 Stroke never made it though. They slogged away in the pubs and clubs and eventually split up. The whole pub circuit apprenticeship for bands was an anachronism in the North East. Too many old fashioned ideas.

Chris Donald

The Cooperage experience

Newcastle's music scene was still in rude health at the start of the 1980s, and I always regarded the Cooperage as its focal point. There were many pubs in and around the city where you could catch a band playing live, but nowhere else with a late licence, dancing facilities and a regular crowd regardless of who was on.

The Cooperage was perfectly suited to the business of creating a scene. It had three connecting rooms: a bar with a pool table for those who simply wanted a late drink, a larger one for general hanging out, and a dark and sweat-drenched cellar where the bands played and the dancing was done. Of course it wasn't a cellar, but after a few pints the bare stone walls and low beams gave the impression of being deep underground. Which is quite remarkable, considering the venue was on the top floor of an ancient and rickety building on the Quayside.

The secret of its success was having resident bands that cultivated their own large followings over a period of time. This had worked well elsewhere since the sixties and one of the most popular bands at The Cooperage was the Junco Partners, reliving their residency at the Club a'GoGo, 15 years

Top, Marshall Hall, left, and Hot Snax, at the Cooperage.

earlier. All the bands that played there were ones you could dance to after a few bevvies. So the more precious and avant garde acts with synths and drum machines never fared well, which is maybe why the venue isn't remembered by some as the coolest or hippest of its time.

I played bass guitar in Hot Snax and we did Monday nights in 1980 – switching to Thursdays later in the year – and our brand of post-industrial European reggae seemed to do the trick. We'd pull a couple of hundred or so on top of the regular clientèle, rotating the support bands to relieve the tedium of having to dance to the same dozen songs as last week. I'd also go on nights when we weren't playing there to check out the competition, great local bands such as the Sabre Jets, Young Bucks, Neon, Disguise and White Heat.

It was Arthur 2 Stroke & The Chart Commandos who took The Cooperage experience to a whole new level. They had a big soul sound pumped up further with a brass section, and a pair of bongos for extra rhythm. One of the great spectacles of early eighties nightlife was seeing the entire audience drop to the floor and begin paddling

Arthur 2 Stroke performs at Newcastle Poly at a benefit for the miners, 1985.

furiously, when the band launched into their trademark *Theme From Hawaii Five-O*. The queue on Thursday nights stretched along the Quay as far as Julie's nightclub, and I can't think of any band and venue, before or since, that were such a perfect fit for each other.

Their stint at The Cooperage lasted a couple of years, till about 1982. Although bands continued to play there throughout the decade, the tradition of residencies pretty much died out. Hot Snax released a single towards the end of 1980, but we split up shortly afterwards when the songwriter and driving force, Steve Foley, moved to London. I played in a couple of bands after this but support for local music dropped dramatically, as specialist club nights began to appear where you could enjoy good music, a dance and a late drink; and scenes could be more cheaply and conveniently developed by a bloke with a box of records.

Marshall Hall

The East Side Torpedoes and beyond

Steve pictured in On the Town, *1983.*

I left school in 1981 and began helping out the East Side Torpedoes having got to know the band at their gigs at the Gosforth Assembly Rooms and the legendary Sunday residency at The Playhouse. I ended up roadying for them and became very friendly with drummer Dave Allen. I played drums myself. They were doing well; there were a lot of music shows featuring local bands, such as the late-night *Friday Live*, on local TV. Attendances were getting bigger, the band was gaining momentum, it was all moving in the right direction. One day they were due to play at Darlington Arts Centre and the call came that Dave (who had some health issues) couldn't make the gig. I'd been hanging about for so long that I knew the set inside out, so they asked me to play. After about a year I became a full-time member, often both playing and roadying.

Chas Chandler produced our only album. Unfortunately it didn't turn out as well as expected but it was well received by the band's followers. I remember walking down into town past the student halls of residence, or past houses in Jesmond and hearing it being played a lot. The band decided we were doing well enough at festivals and in London, so maybe we could make it, but we were quite naïve. Over time it became evident that the band was a bit unwieldy (nine musicians and three roadies) to make a living doing gigs and the recording industry had moved on to other sounds.

We'd get around 400 people every Sunday morning in the Playhouse; the Buddle Arts Centre was a regular Thursday gig; Gosforth on a Tuesday; we played the Lonsdale occasionally although it was a tight squeeze! We had regular gigs in universities and colleges but my favourites were our trips to Dingwalls in Camden, all very exciting for a youngster. It was almost a living but then I didn't have the heavy burden of the usual bills, mortgage etc!

I left the Torpedoes and joined Prefab Sprout in 1983. That was very different but the songs were great. We toured with Elvis Costello. In 1984 I joined a Liverpool based band called The Tempest and toured with Squeeze a couple of times. It was all a great experience and I got to work with some great people too. I consider myself fortunate to still be making a living as a musician 32 years later.

Steve Dolder

Rock impresario

In 1981 local legend Brendan Foster and I were discussing ways to widen the use of Gateshead Stadium and we came up with the idea of the first ever Tyneside two-day rock festival. Roxy Music let me down, but I finally booked Ian Dury and the Blockheads and Elvis Costello to headline day one and Rory Gallagher to headline day two. Local fans had just seen Lindisfarne and would be doing so again at the Christmas shows but they also appeared along with many other bands including a group with a building reputation called U2. Almost 15,000 people attended the festival, which made it by far the biggest music festival ever held in the North East. It put Gateshead and Newcastle on the map. The following year U2 appeared again, along with The Police, and Tyneside has never looked back.

That same year it was pure luck that I grabbed the opportunity to bring Sammy Cahn to Newcastle for a three-day visit to raise money for the Variety Club children's charity. Hardly anyone on the Variety Club

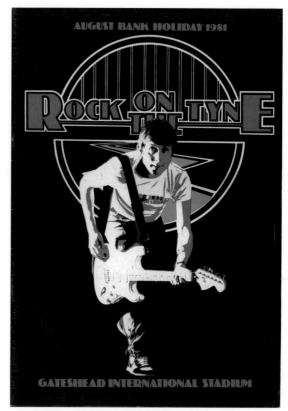

committee had heard of the man who co-wrote many of Frank Sinatra's best known hits, film music and show tunes but after I had enthused about the potential for a Hollywood-style show business event, the committee agreed to hold a tribute dinner for Sammy on a Saturday night followed by a headlining show at the Theatre Royal on Sunday 4 October 1981, then a late-night dinner and show at the Gosforth Park hotel. I also arranged for Sammy to present the keys at our latest Variety Club sunshine coach handover. He loved Newcastle and said the Theatre Royal was the best venue he had ever performed in.

The following year the BBC held their first ever two-day Radio One Fun Weekend in Newcastle's Exhibition Park. Newcastle had never seen anything quite like the event on 5 June. The Variety Club's local members organised a fairground and catering … we had a main arena, a three-ring circus, the Radio One Road Show, parachuting/helicopters/Skyfever aerobatics, fashion shows and 10 acts playing live each day. There was a human juke box, Marvo the Magician, Beat the Gunfighter, a disco, video games, wishing wells, tombola, Deathriders motorcycle stunt team, a high wire act, axe racing, a human cannon ball, racing camels, numerous side stalls and the 'Variety Club celebrity Tent' where people paid 20p admission to obtain celebrity autographs and photos with the stars. Chaos was caused by the arrival of Haircut 100. The band had a fanatical teenage following – their tour coach couldn't get into the park as it was swamped with fans banging on the windows the moment it was spotted. Then there were so many people surrounding the coach the band couldn't get out safely. With the help of the police we somehow got the band into the celebrity tent. How the tent remained standing was beyond me.

Barry McKay

In 1982 the hugely popularBucks Fizz also raised money for the Variety Club. Barry McKay is far left.

My best 80s gigs

Devo at the City Hall (6 May 1980) – wearing white lab coats and strange metal helmets, robotic movement, people surging to the front of the seats. Reworkings of classics like *Working in a Coal Mine* and *Satisfaction*.

The wonderful cool alto saxist Lee Konitz at the Corner House, playing with John Taylor on piano (11 May 1986). The knee jiggling count was off the radar and my devotion was such that the next day I ran out and purchased my very own Lee Konitz checked jacket and sandals (no socks, of course). These distinctive sartorial accoutrements I still have and occasionally wear for special occasions.

NCJ / Mirrorpix

The sartorial elegance of Heaton's Corner House in 1986.

Several Ray Stubbs gigs at the Corner House, usually with his All Stars. Wonderful urban blues and they really put in a shift as the football commentators say.

The eccentric Slim Gaillard at the Corner House (12 Oct 1982) with his hip invented language. He even signed my LP, adding '*vout*' after his signature (ask your groovy dad if you don't know what it means).

Several improv gigs in 1980 at Spectro Arts Centre, featuring such luminaries as Lol Coxhill and David Toop. I remember Steve Beresford with his array of musical toys, particularly since I saw him recently at the Sage in a tribute to Kurt Schwitters with what looked like the same toys. Now he looks like everybody's favourite uncle which certainly was not the case then.

Finally, and stretching a geographical point, my wife and I went on a bus with a cheery load of rock n' rollers to see the incomparable Bo Diddley at a club in Sunderland called, I think, Close Encounters (18 Feb 1982). It was a night of repetition with that shuffling chugging beat taking over everything and everybody as Bo, his rectangular guitar and his glamorous backing singers did the business. I think he even wore his famous check jacket (much louder than Lee's, of course) and cowboy hat. It was a subdued but sated trip back.

Returning to Tyneside, I have a note of a gig of which I have absolutely no recollection: seen on 9 Feb 1982, White Heat at the Hofbrauhaus (can't even remember where it was). Checking on YouTube I discover that they were a punk group who had a hit called *Nervous Breakdown*. The lead singer, stripped to the waist, did press ups on stage, and everything was very loud. Did I really go? If I did, was I asleep for some reason? Or have I just got a very bad memory? If so, can you really trust any of the above?

Peter Hodgkiss

Lynx Studios

When my ex-husband Brian Johnson landed the job of lead singer with heavy rock band AC/DC in 1980, life as we knew it changed forever.

It was a whirlwind, from rags to riches, like lottery winners. From a little semi in North Shields to a huge house in Jesmond Park West in a matter of months. Brian had been in a band called Geordie, which had a small taste of success in the 70s, with a few performances on *Top of the Pops* and regular gigs in northern social clubs to packed audiences after that. I was doing jobs ranging from bingo calling, collecting for the Provi and making car door trims in a

Carol Macdonald

Carol and Brian Johnson, 1980.

factory. Brian always fancied the idea of having his own recording studio so when he switched to AC/DC we bought Lynx Studios in Shieldfield and added De-Luca to the name in honour of Brian's Italian mam.

Lynx took off straight away because of Brian and the AC/DC connection and did really well. After we divorced, I took over the running of the studio full time with engineer John Craig Aitcheson, and later with Mond Cowie from the Angelic Upstarts. We got loads of business from Tyne Tees TV, who were broadcasting *The Tube* and *Roxy* live from their studios on City Road, and most of the artists appearing on those shows came to Lynx to record their backing tracks to comply with Musicians Union rules. It kept us in business for years. We also had Chubby Brown recording his stuff regularly and even the kids from the TV series *Byker Grove* came in to record the theme song – maybe Ant & Dec were there.

Carol Macdonald

This is me with Jimmy Nail outside Lynx at the time of the first Comic Relief in 1985. We raised loads of money charging people a pound a time to come in to the recording booth and tell Jimmy a joke! He did a great job, stayed all day and all he got for his trouble was a few cups of tea! He was starring in 'Auf Wiedersein, Pet!' at the time so was a huge draw. Eddie Kidd, the stunt rider, was also in Newcastle and I gave him one of Brian's gold discs to take to Tyne Tees Television and auction live on the programme. (Carol Macdonald)

Ronnie Lambert, a local singer and song-writer (he wrote *The Toon Anthem*), was always on the lookout for backers to pay for his recording sessions and I suggested he contact author Catherine Cookson. He did, and she paid his recording bill! What a lady!

Brian wasn't around much in those days because of his commitments with AC/DC but John, Mond and I got on with it and we had some fun, I can tell you! We started special deals with London-based record companies to send their budding talent to Lynx instead of paying the high prices of southern studios. We also introduced cheap all-night sessions for just £12 an hour – everyone could afford to record at that price. We ventured into the publishing side of music with an in-house song writer pitching songs to well-known artists. The biggest name to make the trip to Newcastle was Alvin Stardust.

Lynx was a pretty sophisticated studio for the time, but soon more and more people were discovering all sorts of gadgetry and computers that enabled them to record in their bedroom for nowt. That was when Lynx stopped earning its keep. Fortunately Chas Chandler brought a lot of work our way. He had found unheard tapes of Jimi Hendrix and wanted to remix them and re-produce them for an album. It was all very hush-hush as there was some sort of legal wrangle going on in the USA with Jimi's family and copyright so Chas wouldn't let the tapes out of his sight. He even brought the original Experience, Noel Reading and Mitch Mitchel, to the studio to record. It was surreal having them in the studio in the dead of night and Hendrix's voice coming through as though he was also there.

I was involved in Geordie Aid in 1985, and also with a players versus rockstars charity snooker tournament to raise funds for policewoman Maureen Martin who had been shot while on duty. It was at this event I first met Alex 'Hurricane' Higgins and we remained good friends.

Before Lynx I owned one of the first video rental shops in Newcastle – Roxy Video on Shields Road. My only competition was Nationwide on Clayton Street, which was owned by Norma Dunn, Freddie Shepherd's sister. In those days people had to pay to be a member of a video shop and my first member, registered as my No. 1 was a certain Mr J. Milburn who, as customer No. 1, was given a year's free membership. When Brian popped in to see how the first day of trading had gone, he looked in the book and said, 'Mr J. Milburn … Could that be the one and only footballer, Jackie Milburn?' Brian was a huge fan of Jackie (as is my present husband Malcolm Macdonald) and anything to do with Newcastle United. The next day he was lurking around in the back shop waiting for Mr J. Milburn to return his tape and sure enough Jackie came in and I asked him if he was THAT Jackie Milburn, he said yes and I shouted, 'Yep! It's him Brian, for God's sake come out and say hello!'

Carol Macdonald

Carol Macdonald

BRIAN JOHNSON · JOHN MILES · TIM HEALEY · RAY LAIDLAW · MICK WHITAKER · STEVE DAGGETT
IAN McCALLUM · CHARLIE HARCOURT · MIKE WALLER · ALAN HULL · STUART COLLINGWOOD
· RAY JACKSON · OLGA · RON SOLOMON · IAN CAMPBELL · KEVIN RIDLEY · RICHARD DENTON ·
ALAN ROBSON · CHRIS COWEY · ALASTAIR PIRRIE · MIKE NEVILLE · IRENE CURREN · ANNE ORWIN
· VAL McLANE · SUSAN DENT · IRENE HUME · BREN LAIDLER · MELANIE TEASDALE · BEVV BLACK ·
DECCA WADE · MOND COWIE · ROD CLEMENTS · BOB BARTON · HILTON VALENTINE · AILSA HALL
· RONNIE BRYANT · LINDA FERGUSON · IAN SUTHERLAND · NEIL McDONALD · STEVIE ROSS ·
WES SAUNDERS · BOB TAYLOR · BRIAN TEASDALE · JIMMY MOORE · BOB HARRISON · BRIAN HUME
· MARTY CRAGGS · TERRY O HERN · LINDOLPH DE OLIVEIRA · GEOFF STEVENS · DAVID WOOD ·
KEITH NICHOL · ROYSTON MAYO · BARRIE SPENCE · JOHN HUTTON · PAUL CAMPBELL · BILL KEITH
IAN VARDY · JED GRIMES · MICKY DICK · RACHEL NEWTON · PETER BEARDSLEY · KENNY WHARTON
· SHARON BIBBY · CLIVE TAYLOR · MAVIE HALES · CAROL JOHNSON · STEVE BOWN · MRS PIRRIE ·
· RAY GRAHEN · LES GILFILLAN · EILEEN MILES · DAVY BASS JNR · DAVY BASS · HELP 01

Spot the star on the City Hall stage. Geordie Aid, Newcastle's answer to Band Aid, was recorded at the famous Impulse Studios in Wallsend in 1985. It included many well-known national and local performers. (Christopher Baglee's book: 'Impulse Studios, 40 Years of Recording Rock on Tyneside' is in preparation.)

City Road, Tyne Tees TV studios and two of the pubs where the stars, the punters, and the crew of The Tube drank. The Egypt Cottage, on the right, was nicknamed Studio 6. The whole building – the whole of City Road – was buzzing.

DANCING IN THE STREET

David Bowie, Mick Jagger, 1985

THE TUBE and the people that made it happen

Alright Now aired on Tyne Tees TV from December 1979 to August 1980 and was the first music show I produced. We recorded it as a live gig in a TV studio at a time when standard music fare on TV was like *Top of the Pops* where the band mimed, the audience bopped around a set, and the presenters were usually DJs from the BBC or commercial radio. The whole thing tended to be very bland.

Our audience was allowed to do whatever they wanted, like at a gig … drink, dance, pogo, snog … they could do it. The bands had a proper sound check, and, controversially, we let their sound guys actually operate a desk, which, at a time when unions were very, very powerful in television, was revolutionary stuff. And very quickly we started attracting some really big names. The Clash, who famously never ever did TV and hated *ToTP* with a passion, only did two TV shows in their entire career – and one of them was *Alright Now*.

When Channel 4 came along in 1982, Jeremy Isaacs, a brilliant visionary man who was passionate about breaking the monopoly of London and the cartel of the major ITV companies, decided every show on the channel would be fully networked, and he welcomed programmes that weren't from London. So here was a great opportunity. My boss, Andrea Wonfor, and her boss, Andy Allan, and I came up with the idea of a show like *Alright Now* to pitch to Jeremy. We proposed *Jamming*, six half-hour programmes with a format based on *Alright Now*, but with bands jamming together too.

Channel 4 turned that idea down, BUT they DID want a 20-week music show of one hour 45 minute programmes live from City Road, Newcastle. The budget ran to seven figures. And they wanted it to start the week Channel 4 went on air, on Bonfire Night. Jeremy told us: 'there are only two things I want to say to you … make it LIVE and give it BALLS!' That was the commission.

We advertised for presenters in *The Face*, the coolest magazine on the planet: 'Wanted: a Face for the Space' and a telephone number. We got over 1,000 phone applications. We wanted to give the coolest, brand new people an opportunity to show their passion and their love for music, so that's how we got people like Muriel Grey and the other guys. Jarvis Cocker came from Sheffield in a little red mini for an interview. Boy George (who arrived in a wedding dress) would have got the show if he hadn't been signed up by Virgin Records. We finally settled on Jools and Paula. Jools had presented on a great documentary about The Police in Montserrat – really off the wall – this is the boy for us!

Our pilot show was a complete disaster. We were still recording it at 1am, clocking up a huge amount of studio time and it really was a shambles, but we finally went on air on 5 November1982 with The Jam's last ever last performance, Billy Bragg, and Pete Townsend from The Who, and it was fantastic.

Elaine Cusack

We gave out a Punter's Pass to selected people so they could get in every week and the queues went right round the entire block. One day I got called down by the Chief Inspector of Newcastle Constabulary and he said 'Malcolm, this has got to stop, we've got 600 people out there'. Most of them had been there all night and he was worried about health and safety. We didn't have room for a huge audience, probably 100 max, but we ran and ran so most people managed to get in at some point.

It became quite a Mecca for talent and we started getting enquiries from Canada, New Zealand, Holland, all the countries that the programme sold to. One year 30 people from Germany turned up and I remember Jools making a crack on air like 'Don't mention the war'. We were commissioned to film U2 at the Red Rocks gig in Colorado in 1983. And we sold that concert to something like 85 countries world wide. BA had to change their last flight to London on a Friday night. It used to take off at 6.50pm but they realised they were missing out on people that had been on *The Tube* and were having to get the train back to London instead, so after the first series they moved the flight to 8pm. When the series finished Nova Taxis laid off more than 20 drivers.

Tina Turner was a highlight. We had booked her to do three songs and the programme was due to go off air at 7pm. At 7.50 she was still performing and she was amazing! Annie Lennox was in the audience dancing like crazy. The cameramen and some of the electricians, who weren't really into this sort of thing, were just dancing along with the audience. It was like having a very private gig with one of the greatest female artistes of all time. She was just one of many many fine acts.

Malcolm Gerrie, Senior Producer

The Tube: Eddi Reader with Annie Lennox and Dave Stewart of Eurythmics. (Photo ITV / Rex Features)

On 5 November 1982 Channel 4 hit the TV screens of Britain. A low-key broadcast of *Countdown*, fronted by the urbane Richard Whiteley, was followed by a not so urbane Jools Holland waving a sparkler in front of Tyne Tees Television's futuristic tunnel entrance to Studio 5. *The Tube* was upon us! Andrea Wonfor accurately described it as 'not so much a TV programme – more of an attitude'. And attitude it had; it was a perfect mirror of the narcissistic, video-friendly, ironic, style-laden music scene of the 80s. Most importantly it was not London-centric, which meant that for five years Newcastle was a capital of TV cool. In some ways it helped to herald the city's cultural regeneration.

Madonna made her TV debut on *The Tube*. Warners didn't pay her return rail expenses – so we gave her £37 in cash in a buff expenses envelope.

The very first band to play on *The Tube* was The Toy Dolls, singing a song that paid homage to a Sunderland wine bar, Fino's.

THE very last band to play were Duran Duran but it was supposed to be James Brown. I had worked for eight weeks through a Swiss promoter

Chris on the set of The Tube with Robin George, editor of Kerrang Geoff Barton, and Cronos. The Tube catered for many musical tastes!

to get him – but in the end he cancelled due to dental problems so EMI flew Duran in from Belfast.

Frankie Goes To Hollywood were discovered by accident – the crew actually went to film Dead or Alive in Liverpool but they couldn't be found. A barman recommended this other band that was rehearsing round the corner so *The Tube* crew filmed the original line-up, including the Leatherpets, performing the original *Relax* with an extra verse. Their Grammy award winning producer, Trevor Horne, hailed from County Durham.

The Egypt Cottage was nicknamed Studio 6. Some visitors dropped in for a drink one day, and, propped against the bar, was Ozzy Osbourne, standing in an upright coffin, accompanied by Sharon. They were waiting for an interview. The visitors drank VERY quickly and left.

The Tube, City Road and Paula Yates are all sadly gone, but the attitude remains!

Chris Phipps, Assistant Producer

Top, Billy Bragg and Bono at the end of the first series.
Above, Chris, film editor Peter Bensimon and Little Richard.

On my first day working on *The Tube* at Tyne Tees my union ticket was checked four times. I realised this wasn't going to be an easy ride! The crew of *The Tube* was thought to have privileges including going abroad a lot on location. We'd get dirty looks in the canteen.

It didn't help that cameraman Graham Brown might arrive with me in the Rose and Crown on a Friday night with the studio camera crew and remark 'Oh where do you fancy going next week? D'you fancy going to Jamaica?' The looks we got! But then we had a very particular job to do, and we brought back fantastic footage from these trips. For instance when we filmed Boy George and Culture Club in Japan it was on the front cover of the *TV Times* before we'd even shot it. We worked 16-hour days, but we loved it. The pressure came off me then as the other directors just didn't want to know about work loads like that.

We didn't mind any member of the crew being in shot if they looked interested. We had created a style and everyone loved it. It was all hand held. People didn't do interviews hand held then, but I said 'break the vision', for instance when Mick Jagger came to be interviewed on *The Tube* sofa I put the camera between him and Jools. Mick did get bashed on the head, but didn't bat an eyelid.

The classic band discovery was Frankie Goes To Hollywood who we filmed, by chance really, in Liverpool. *Relax* was the best produced song of the 80s. Three weeks later it was in the charts, and when the BBC banned it, it went berserk. *Then* we had them to play live in the studio!

Sarah Hall

We were nearly banned many times, not just when Jools said the F word. The nudity! We filmed a band called Naughty Miranda. She was just dressed in a bin bag and had a fantastic figure and eyes. I shot it half in the studio and half in a padded cell … The words started 'I've just killed my father…'. This was going out at teatime … it went down very well!

One time Jools and Paula were waiting to be filmed outside *The Tube* on a freezing cold night. They had the mikes on and Channel 4 came on air early with a screen saying '*The Tube* follows shortly'. Oh dear, all you can hear is Jools saying 'By god it's cold,' followed by Paula saying 'It's f…g freezing! My tits are falling off!'. Once they realised they were being recorded Jools says 'My, it's jolly cold out here!'

It was all a bit anarchic but in a good rock n' roll way. We smashed all the rules. We didn't have time to get clearance for all the clips we had. It was seven days a week, and when you weren't doing it you were thinking about it.

Geoff Wonfor, Tube Film Director

My area of responsibility was Associate Producer Non-Music Items – a bit of a challenge on what was very much a music show. However, the commissioner from Channel 4, Mike Bolland, insisted that we needed to include other items in order to reflect the whole of 'young modern culture' in the way that *The Face* magazine did.

We focused on comedy, which included people like Rik Mayall, Robbie Coltrane, the *Spitting Image* puppets and Dame Edna Everage. It was a risky strategy but at the same time was highly successful. Regular visitors were two very young comedians, Dawn French and Jennifer Saunders, who played 'punters' and 'Jools's biggest fans'. I used to ring Dawn French each week to discuss what they were going to do on the next programme. Her ansaphone messages were always a treat! The most memorable one was a spoof of her and Lenny Henry together, as if the call had interrupted them having sex! Dawn and Jennifer were always very close to the edge in terms of what was acceptable on TV. Remember we were going out 5.30 – 7pm and there are strict rules about what can be said and done at this time, plus the show was live. Dawn and Jennifer's characters developed from being 'fans in the audience' until Jools allowing them to try a bit of presenting. This of course led to total chaos. So Jools 'sacked them on air' and Dawn shouted up to him 'How can you do this to us, Jools? Remember the blow-job I gave you earlier?!' There was horror in the control box and at Channel 4. I was hauled into the boss's office to explain how this could happen. But we all knew, there was really no way to avoid it.

The Tube became famous for this sort of gaffe. At one point I was given the job of trying to keep Paula Yates on track – again, not easy to achieve. Seconds before going on air one week, we were standing outside the Studio where Paula was due to open the programme, and she was chatting about the incredible size of a particular rock star's private parts – in graphic detail. None of us knew the sound was turned up and being beamed out to the nation! Just another fun moment in the history of *The Tube*.

Lesley Oakden, Associate Producer

Unpredictable presenter Paula Yates with Dave Stewart of Eurythmics on location for The Tube in Los Angeles.

Jimmy Forsyth was interviewed on *The Tube*. He was brilliant! He was a real character, very much a Tube-type person … passionate, a bit eccentric. He took some stunning photos. One of those people who comes along once in a lifetime and manages to capture something magical. Jools was quite black and white about who he liked or didn't like and Jimmy was definitely in the like category.

Malcolm Gerrie

1980 saw me starting a new job as a location sound recordist. I'd worked in the studio sound department at Tyne Tees TV for six years and, having decided to apply to try life on the road, was looking forward to filming the likes of *Farming Outlook*, *Sportstime*, current affairs documentary items about being a hill shepherd and so forth. Eighteen months on the adrenaline started pumping when our crew of five found out that we were to be filming location reports for the new Channel 4 rock show: *The Tube*. Talk about the deep end! 'First shoot is in Glasgow followed by a special report from LA.'

What an adventure for four Geordies and a token Yorkshire tyke! This was, technically and logistically, quite a challenge for me on sound – it was a music show after all. I do remember going to Disneyland on our rest day and sending a postcard back to Tyne Tees saying 'We've found another Mickey Mouse outfit out here!' We must have done alright as a few months later we were sent to do a special on Duran Duran, mega at the time, in the South of France. I'm the one in the photo with knees bent, no idea why. Shortly after that film went out I was recognized a couple of times when out shopping. It turned out that one of the fashion stores on Northumberland Street had taped the show and was playing it on a loop on large screens. In the opening sequence I'd been filmed with Jools Holland as he spoke to camera. He was on an escalator and this had been a quick and 'creative' solution to recording his voice while attached to my recorder by a cable. Fame at last!

Nic Grant, crew sound recordist

Nic Grant, fourth from the left with bent legs, on location with the crew in the south of France with Duran Duran, 1983. Geoff Wonfor, film director, is centre back with a beard.

Tiffanys ran an alternative night called A Packet of Cornflakes … don't ask me why! One night (it must have been 1982) I was dancing there with a friend and a couple of guys, who might have had cameras, came up and said they were looking for people to appear on a new TV programme … and could we come along and dance, wearing exactly what we were wearing that night?

The show was *The Tube*. We'd heard of Jools Holland and Paula Yates but we didn't know about *The Tube*. So we turned up at Tyne Tees and we couldn't believe how fantastic it was. There was a bar for soft drinks and all the different stages set up. It was just brilliant … we saw any band you can mention, not just alternative, including BB King.

I was given a punters pass so I never had to queue or audition to be a dancer. People were so jealous, because they'd have to queue for tickets on a Friday afternoon and we'd just march straight to the front of the queue and walk right in. We got to know Jools and Paula, and, when Paula left, Muriel Gray and Lesley Ash were so nice. I'd have to get ready at college to be there for 5pm. We went to almost every show, and we danced wherever they

wanted us to. I sat next to Bono in the green room! Most people were really friendly.

There was a three-hour special featuring the Damned at *The Tube* one week. They didn't show it all on TV. You didn't ever see the whole two hours of *The Tube*. I didn't see it at all because I was there of course. We didn't have a video. It was very exciting if someone *had* videoed it. Marc Almond had a temper tantrum one day as his mike had feedback. He threw it down and stormed off stage.

On Christmas Eve 1984 you could go as your favourite popstar so I went as Debbie Harry. I wore a bin liner (that was easy) and my boyfriend went as Boy George. I added another bin liner up my arms to look like long gloves. All I had on was a bra and knickers, stocking and suspenders, and a bin liner, so by the end of the evening and all the dancing, there wasn't much left of the bin liner. My poor father was picking us up as there were no buses or Metro. I had had to be wrapped in Affaz's jacket and someone else's jumper round my waist. I should have taken a spare binbag. That was a funny night. There were quite a few Debbie Harrys and Boy Georges I remember.

After the very last *Tube* in 1986 there was a party at the Trent, and everyone was there. There was a lock in.

Karen Laidler, punter

The famous entrance to Studio 5, 1983. (Photo ITV / Rex Features)

The Tube blew BBC music programming out of the water with its futuristic theme tune, blend of live and pre-recorded performances, irreverent yet in-depth interviews plus the chemistry between presenters Paula Yates and Jools Holland.

I was thrilled by the show's energy, content and the fact it was made locally. I had a tenuous connection to *The Tube*. One of the girls in my class at school was the daughter of director, Gavin Taylor. Claire was very generous, handing out tickets to classmates but that wasn't enough for this music-obsessed teen. I needed to be in the audience every week.

One early Sunday evening in January 1984 I was dancing with my mate Sharon at Tiffanys under 18's disco when I was approached by a woman. She worked on *The Tube* and invited me to audition for a place in the show's regular audience. I was excited and proud. Clearly my innovative dance interpretation of *White Lines* by Grandmaster Flash had impressed a TV researcher!

I was weeks away from my 14th birthday and I knew I had to be 16 to be an audience member. The researcher hadn't asked my age and I certainly didn't tell my parents about the age limit when they drove me to Tyne Tees for the Tuesday evening audition. As I walked up the famous tube-shaped entrance of Studio 5, wearing my favourite polka dot top from Attic, I knew I looked the part but would I get the gig?

I joined a TV studio full of would-be audience members and we were told to start dancing. Luckily for me they played *White Lines* plus songs by my favourite band, The Smiths. I danced my plimsolls off and wasn't surprised when I was picked as an audience member. Now I'd get to be involved in my favourite show every week!

It was hard work getting to Tyne Tees for 5pm every Friday. I used to scamper home after school finished at 3.45pm to get changed and eat something then Dad would drive me from Felling to City Road. I'd flounce up the entrance past the line of ticket holders for that evening's show, flash my Punter's Pass and gain access to the coolest nightspot in town.

Punters headed to Studio 5 where we'd be briefed on who was playing that evening and when.

Regular audience members were expected to dance, look like we were enjoying ourselves and clap and cheer the bands.

I recall a bar in the corner of the studio serving free soft drinks and think it was researcher Chris Cowey (later a *Top of the Pops* producer) who was the resident DJ playing music to get us in the mood. He usually played *Rock The Casbah* by The Clash and Prince's *1999* as dry ice was pumped into the tiny studio.

I loved watching the show take shape: production staff running around, cameramen zooming in on exotic stage sets as the rest of the audience filed in to what looked like a New York music venue.

The list of bands I saw over the years reads like a *Smash Hits* yearbook: ABC, Frankie Goes to Hollywood, the Eurythmics, Madness and the Cure. I saw Tina Turner making her comeback with *Heaven 17* and marvelled at the late, great Divine crashing down a metal staircase in huge heels singing 'You think you're a man but you're only a boy!' I saw my beloved Smiths more than once and yes, I saw myself on screen several times. One of these occasions was when The Housemartins performed *Caravan of Love* for the first time. I was thrilled when my mate Hugh, the band's drummer, spotted me and came over to say hello before they launched into their acappella set. Dad would usually pick me up just after 7pm and I'd go home to watch the show on video. I reckon my Punter's Pass expired in late 1985.

In 1991 my friend Kim gave me a book about *The Tube* for my 21st birthday. I screeched with horror and delight when I spotted myself in the audience in front of Alison Moyet.

Elaine Cusack, punter

Nicola Booth

I got onto *The Tube* when I was working at the Jubilee. The pub attracted all the rock people, the roadies, and people working in TV. Chris Cowey, one of the people who started *The Tube* came in and announced they were filming a new programme and did anyone fancy a punters pass? So we went every week for that series. We saw everyone from Twisted Sister to Dave Stewart and Michael Hutchence. We met loads of people, just about everyone. It was like going to the pub, the atmosphere was so relaxed. We'd go to Egypt Cottage beforehand, which was probably a mistake, then pile into *The Tube*. When I went away to university in 1983 I came back every week for *The Tube* on the bus. The fare was £5. I got my gold punters pass.

Nicola Booth, punter

This photo is of me and Iggy Pop outside *The Tube* … he had just signed an autograph and I was a bit awestruck. I was a regular at *The Tube*. I was 15 or 16 and me and my friend Tracey used to leave school a bit early on a Wednesday and queue for tickets, not for the coming Friday but the one after. If we could we went every Friday, if we weren't grounded! You weren't supposed to get in under 16 years old and I always looked younger than I was, but they still let the bairns in. I wasn't at the opening but I remember seeing Soft Cell and touching Marc Almond's foot. In those days the stage was very close, and I drank the water he had on stage. I told Mam and she went mad! 'Anything could have been in there' she said, but it was just water. I saw the B52s and Culture Club and many other bands

Paula Ginger, fan

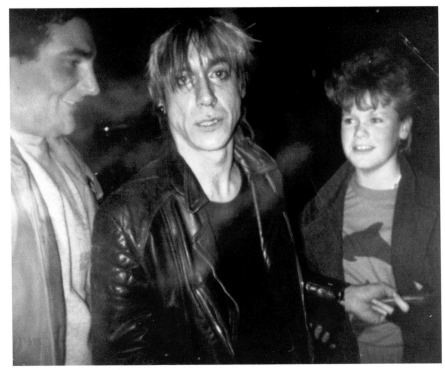

Paula Ginger

Iggy Pop disappeared before his live performance, until reception phoned me to report 'a mummy' wandering in The Tube entrance on City Road – yes it was Mr Pop himself swathed in bandages! (Chris Phipps)

From 1975 until 1988, Badge Group Design was the leading graphic design studio in Newcastle and the Tyne Tees PR department commissioned us to do the launch poster for *The Tube*. At the launch I was probably wearing my favourite green, white and yellow vertical striped silk shirt and baggy topped green tapered trousers with tan pointed shoes – very stylish! Studio 5 was incredibly crowded and the atmosphere was electrifying, with no-one knowing what would be happening next, and whether all of the advertised acts would have time to appear – very exciting!

Christopher Baglee, graphic designer

Above, the 1982 launch poster for The Tube, which was designed in Newcastle by Badge Group Design.

Left, the chrome and enamel lapel badge that each guest was presented with on the launch night.

The *Tube* was great and it's a shame everything connected with it is gone now … the TTTV studios, Egypt Cottage, the Rose and Crown over the road. Artists travelled great distances to be on the show. If you weren't working you'd watch the show before you did anything else. It put the North East on the map. Iggy Pop and many other major iconic names would appear, they'd go out to the clubs in town, so that meant they were on the scene too.

Steve Dolder

No more Tube, July 1988.

We were amazed we got commissioned for a second series never mind a fifth! There were some disasters, including Jools swearing … it has become apocryphal that that incident ended the show, but it's not true. He was just suspended for six weeks. The reason the show ended in 1987 was due to a combination of factors: Channel 4 management and Tyne Tees had changed. They wanted to cut costs and there wasn't same passion for music. I was determined the show should not fizzle out and wither and die like *The Old Grey Whistle Test*, so we decided to end on a high … U2 wrote a song especially for the last show. We were all sad, but the party went on for three days.

Malcolm Gerrie

It was a big trip to visit the grandparents – a train journey from Peterborough then a ride on the new Metro. All very exciting for our two-year-old daughter. As the Metro crossed over Ouseburn to Byker there appeared a pig in the sky! She was absolutely mesmerised and repeated with giggly delight for the rest of the day, 'I saw a pig in the sky' to everybody who would listen. After that anything could happen in this magical place called Tyneside! We never found out why the pig was there but it made its way into our family memories.

Sue Giles

Mystery solved, a pig hovers over the roof of Tyne Tees TV for The Tube Midsummer Night's Party, 1983.
(Photo ITV / Rex Features)

KARMA CHAMELEON

Culture Club, 1983

Culture City

I loved going to see the Royal Shakespeare Company when they were in Newcastle. They came for several weeks and performed in various theatres across the city. The season starting in March 1987 took place at the Tyne Theatre (as the Theatre Royal was being refurbished), the People's Theatre, and the Gulbenkian Studio. They were performing *Richard II, Romeo and Juliet, Macbeth, A Midsummer Night's Dream* and *The Winter's Tale* at the Tyne Theatre. The People's staged *The Fair Maid of the West, Every Man in his Humour, The Rover* and *The Two Noble Kinsmen*, while the Gulbenkian was the venue for *Worlds Apart, Flight, Country Dancing* and *The Art of Success*. Amongst the cast were Jeremy Irons, Imogen Stubbs, Sean Bean, Niamh Cusack, Michael Kitchen, Jonathan Pryce, Hugh Quarshie, Pete Postlethwaite, Joely Richardson, Simon Russell Beale, Nathaniel Parker, Joe Melia, Imelda Staunton, Henry Goodman, David Troughton, Philip Franks. Amazing!

I arrived at the Tyne Theatre to see *Romeo and Juliet*, starring Sean Bean and Niamh Cusack. I spoke to a lady in the loo who was waiting for the box office to open. She had a coffee while waiting and had started talking to one of the actors in the play who had asked her to have a drink with him after the show. She told me that she would love to go, but was a bit nervous, and asked me if I would go along too. We both enjoyed the performance and met up with the young man and his girlfriend. The young actor was Sean Bean and his girlfriend was Melanie

RSC
Royal Shakespeare Company
1986

Newcastle upon Tyne
9 Feb - 14 March 1987
over 100 performances in three theatres!
TYNE THEATRE
PEOPLE'S THEATRE
GULBENKIAN STUDIO

Box Office: 091 232 2061

supported by NORTHERN ARTS

City of Newcastle upon Tyne

Hill, who was starring in a hit sit-com called *Bread*). So, my claim to fame is that Sean Bean bought me a half of lager! It was one of the best experiences of my life!

Irene Soulsby

For me the 1980s offered some wonderful opportunities to see the Royal Shakespeare Company, The National Theatre, The Royal Ballet and many other companies visiting the city. We were treated to some amazing performances at the Theatre Royal from Ben Kingsley, John Woodvine and Timothy Spall in *The Merry Wives of Windsor*; Sir Ralph Richardson in *Early Days*; Harriet Walter and Juliet Stevenson in *A Midsummer Night's Dream*; Dame Peggy Ashcroft in *All's Well That Ends Well*; and Derek Jacobi in *The Tempest*. Familiar faces from television also trod the boards of the Theatre Royal, including Tom Baker in *Educating Rita*; Ian Lavender in *Run for your Wife*; Kevin Whately playing the lead in *Billy Liar*; Peter Bowles and Richard Wilson in *Some of my Best Friends are Husbands*; and Pat Phoenix and Anthony Booth in *Spider's Web*.

Matthew Kelly moved from being a 'fool' on television to straight acting on the stage appearing in the *Hunchback of Notre Dame* and *The Pied Piper*. In 1988 Dame Edna Everage graced us with her presence leaving some of the audience shocked but most doubled up with laughter and a lucky few receiving a gift of a gladioli.

I was introduced to the New Vic Theatre Company – madcap and hilarious performances of *The Canterbury Tales*, *The Three Musketeers* and *Under Milk Wood*. During the interval of *The Three Musketeers* some of the cast came into the stalls and invited members of the audience to join them on stage. As my mother was sitting at the end of the row she was a prime target and 'Cardinal Richelieu' asked her to dance. Her only comment was that 'Cardinal Richelieu' was definitely in character as the smell of garlic was overpowering!

Hazel Nixon

36 Lime Street Studios

I first met Michael Mould in the summer of 1983. I was looking for cheap workshop space and had heard on the grapevine that he had bought the 'Cluny Bond' and was looking for fellow travellers. I chalked a line at one end of a large open floor, and asked the price. 'Tenner a week' replies Michael, deal done. Over the next year others joined – artists, musicians, actors, potters, all making little money and needing a cheap space to set up their studios and workshops. Michael converted the top floor into a flat for himself and rehearsal rooms, workshops, and an office for his Bruvvers Theatre Co. The open floors of the main part of the building were piece by piece divided up, everybody building their own spaces. Michael once referred to us rather theatrically as 'the shock troops of urban regeneration'!

The City Council were concerned that a Grade II listed building was being 'converted' in such an 'ad hoc' way and offered us a grant of £100,000 to carry out the works necessary to bring it up to the building regulation standards. A condition of that grant was that we constitute ourselves into a non-profit-making

Under the new portico at 36 Lime Street, 1988. Tim Kendall is at the back, far right.

company whose aims and objectives were to continue to provide affordable workspace. 36 Lime St Ltd was set up in 1986, the same year we won a national award from the RIBA as a good example of what was then known as 'community architecture'. We even had a visit from Prince Charles in 1988!

Most importantly the 36 Street tenants co-operative had negotiated a 99 year lease for the main part of the building that we occupied. This was on the most generous of terms and I remember Michael's solicitor strongly advising him against signing away his interest so categorically. Tenants past, present and future all owe him a debt of gratitude.

Tim Kendall

I set up my glass studio in 1988. Level 4 had already been made into studios on a self-build basis by furniture makers, painters, sculptors, mime artists and a tempeh business. Level 3 was home to theatre groups Puppets and People and Skin and Bones. The regime was very hands-off, which was fantastic We were there because it was cheap, but it was also very exciting. We got to inhabit a Grade II listed building and run our own lives.

When I told people where my studio was, most hadn't heard of it, unless they had been to the City Farm next door, the Ouseburn boat club or the Ship, or they were interested in industrial archaeology – this was the cradle of Newcastle's industrial revolution. The pub and the boat club were original and very local, and the farm was the only sign of regeneration.

I have lovely memories of eating lunch on the grass outside with goats grazing next to us. The Ship Inn was run by Wynne and John with Mel behind the bar and you could have any combination of beans, eggs, sausage, toast and bacon, washed down with a cup of tea. There was lots of music, a free festival on the green every year, and there were warehouse parties. We did a lot of teaching and community workshops. There was a lot of collaboration and experimentation and conversation. We felt very lucky.

Bridget Jones

36 Lime Street, 1989.
Inset, the 'Cluny Bond', 1983.

Newcastle Arts Centre

Newcastle Arts Centre was founded by Mike and Norma Tilley in July 1981. Spectro Arts Workshop had began at Whitley Bay in 1971 and opened a new Centre in Bells Court off Pilgrim Street in 1976. The arts centre at Bell's Court was converted from a former Ryman's showroom and warehouse which extended over three floors to include a gallery, performance space, electronic music studio, screen print workshop, a complete photographic workshop and studios in the basement.

Spectro was originally funded by the experimental arts panel of the Arts Council and later supported by Northern Arts and Newcastle City. The pioneering Bell's Court project helped put Newcastle on the national arts map by employing outstanding young artists and inviting ground-breaking artists to visit and show in Newcastle. This included solo shows by international names such as Richard Hamilton, John Stezaker and Helen Chadwick. It created an interest in contemporary art programming in Newcastle that would pave the way for the Baltic.

Mike and Norma left Spectro in 1980. With planning permission and some funding on offer, Newcastle Arts Centre Limited was formed and the site on Westgate Road was bought. Spectro would later lose its home in Bell's Court, change its name to Newcastle Media Workshop and join the Arts

Mike Tilley

The new Arts Centre under conversion, 1981.

Centre at Westgate Road as Projects UK as an independent tenant.

The site, which was a block of seven abandoned buildings between Westgate Road and Pink Lane, was a mix of old Merchant houses, shops, warehousing and a former department store in one of the oldest parts of central Newcastle. It offered the opportunity for a mixed use development where some buildings could be rented out to help fund the provision of art space with street level access that is integrated into the existing townscape. This happened at a time when government was under pressure to support projects that took on inner city problems.

From the start the project was all about recycling old buildings and maintaining their identity within the community. The MSC job creation programme developed craft skills for the renovation, and grants and funding from Tyne & Wear and Newcastle Councils made it all possible.

Newcastle Arts Centre received a Times RIBA Community Enterprise Award and was the subject of a case study for the Arts and the Changing City Symposium in Glasgow in October 1988. Prince Charles officially opened the Centre in November 1988.

STOP PRESS   STOP PRESS   STOP PRESS   STOP PRESS

TARA ARTS GROUP

From 13th – 25th February Newcastle Arts Centre will be the venue for the Tara Arts Group from London. This Asian Community Theatre Project will feature open rehearsals and workshops culminating in performances from 23rd – 25th February.

Newcastle Arts Centre is a new facility for trade exhibitions, craft fairs, conferences and seminars with a full Theatre and Public Entertainments licence.
We are now open to accept bookings.
We offer a City centre venue, close to the Central Station with excellent ground floor access and public parking at Bath Lane, the Swallow Hotel and the Central Station. If you need to stage a presentation or set up a meeting contact,

Newcastle Arts Centre

67–69 Westgate Road   Phone 261 5618

From Paint it Red, February 1989.

The Centre would finish the decade as the home of professional arts practice in Newcastle accommodating Northern Stage, New Writing North, and Projects UK itself recognised by the Arts Council as a Key Strategic Organisation for Photography, Audio work and Visual Arts productions. The Centre also promoted a successful Edinburgh Fringe StopOver programme and an annual Professional Craft Fair.

Newcastle Arts Centre has operated without revenue grant aid since 1993 and continues to flourish as one of a few independent Art Centres in England, supported by 90,000 visitors per year.

Mike Tilley

Opening time

Heaton in the 80s was opening itself up to the New. It was a golden age, but then again, in those days we *were* the New, buying back furniture cleared from the houses of the deceased to re-furnish the selfsame houses transformed to the New with the floors now stripped and stud walls knocked down. The New was going to be an open plan world. Men-only bars were opening up to women, high streets were opening up to chain stores and minds were opening up to change.

Basil Bunting at home with with Ted Hughes. Opening up the New.

from Basil Bunting: Briggflatts (with CD and DVD) Bloodaxe Books, 2009.

In between fending off the lead strippers and fireplace thieves of Heaton, and working as a full-time sub-editor at the *Evening Chronicle*, I was endeavouring to help a talented young editor called Neil Astley establish Bloodaxe Books and open up British poetry to the New in poetry: Ken Smith, Simon Armitage, Helen Dunmore, Fleur Adcock, C.K. Williams and many more, with the support of Northern Arts, now part of Arts Council England.

Our own minds were opened when Neil and I went to pay homage to the great Northumbrian poet Basil Bunting, then in his 80s and living in Washington New Town. We took him a bottle of whisky with which he promptly filled three glass tumblers before waxing lyrical on mis-translations of the King James Bible, the state of poetry and his famous autobiographical poem, *Briggflatts*, featuring Eric Bloodaxe, 'king of the Orkneys, king of Dublin, twice king of York', from whom Bloodaxe Books takes its name.

If Bunting had written *Briggflatts* to open up the mind of the young Geordie poet Tom Pickard, then Tom and his then-wife Connie had opened up Tyneside to the new poetry of Allen Ginsberg, Lawrence

Ferlinghetti, and many of the world's finest poets, in their famous poetry readings at the mediaeval Morden Tower. Bunting died in 1985.

Bloodaxe, meanwhile, was helping to open up a locked door in Russia, where a 28-year-old poet, Irina Ratushinskaya, was being held in a strict regime labour camp for 'agitation' because of her poetry. She smuggled out new poems on scraps of paper sometimes exchanged in kisses with her husband, Igor, and Bloodaxe published them. The book, *No, I'm Not Afraid*, was presented to Presidents Mikhail Gorbachev and Ronald Reagan. On the eve of the 1986 Reykjavik summit, she was released. Success!

Opening minds was more difficult, as demonstrated by the *Daily Mail*'s 1987 front page banner headline FOUR-LETTER TV POEM FURY after an 'outraged' Tory MP objected to Gosforth poet Tony Harrison's poem *V* ('in which the crudest, most offensive word', was used 17 times) being broadcast on Channel 4.

In 1984, the *Evening Chronicle*, in conjunction with Bloodaxe Books, ran a poetry competition. The picture shows (left to right: the editor of Bloodaxe Books, Neil Astley, myself in a bow tie, the late and much missed Graeme Stanton, and the internationally acclaimed poet Anne Stevenson. What is remarkable is the talent captured in this competition over the years it ran. Several of the winners, including Matthew Caley and Brendan Cleary went on to become established poets. In the junior section, the winner, Colleen Prendergast – then aged 11 and with a broken arm – is now a successful actress.

The public reading by the winners took place in a hot room at the Civic Centre on a sweltering day after Michael

Buerk's harrowing report on the Ethiopian famine that killed a million people which set a new standard in journalism at the time. Like many others that day, we organised a collection and raised a surprising amount. The people of Tyneside were looking to the world, as they always do.

Simon Thirsk

When I was 15 the Central Library was where I explored my new interest in poetry. Inspiration hit me one April evening like a big wet, fish and I started writing a poem a day. It was a very exciting time and I was hungry for poetry. I swallowed anthologies, and fell in love with the work of my very own Fab Four: Philip Larkin, Stevie Smith, Sylvia Plath and ee cummings.

I fell into Newcastle's poetry scene in the autumn of 1985. When the *Evening Chronicle* poetry competition was announced in September, I bombarded the judges with poems. To my delight I was awarded an adult prize: a week-long residential poetry course at the Arvon Foundation's centre in Hebden Bridge but I had to wait until I turned 16 before I could attend.

The *Evening Chronicle* Poetry competition became very important to me. Over the next three years I entered poems and won prizes and developed a relationship with Bloodaxe Books as well as the newspaper. Neil Astley encouraged my poetry and I got to know Simon Thirsk because of his role at Bloodaxe as well as

Cool young poet. Elaine Cusack, 1986.

his 'day job' in the *Evening Chronicle* Features Department. Bloodaxe Books operated out of a cool building on the Quayside. I loved visiting the office after school. It made me feel like I was part of a film set.

Peter Mortimer's Iron Press was another important part of Newcastle's poetry scene. As well as publishing books, Peter produced *Iron* magazine. Other North East magazines at this time included *The Echo Room*, *Stand* and *Writing Women*. Morden Tower was still being used as a poetry venue and I recall performing in a veggie restaurant in Fenham called The Red Herring Café.

Elaine Cusack

Harambe! Africa

From June 1987 the Harambe! Africa festival brought the cream of African music to Newcastle, including the Bhundu Boys, Stella Chiweshe, Thomas Mapfumo, Mahlatini and the Mohatella Queens, Reme Ongala and Ali Farka Toure as well as the world's youngest professional kora player Pa Jobartah who was just 12 years old.

The gigs were held mainly at the Riverside club, which had opened in 1985 and was, despite the absence of a licence in the early days, an immediate and great success. Other venues included the Playhouse, Live Theatre, Blaydon Shopping Centre and old Eldon Square.

With the help of a Northern Arts grant I was able to travel to Zimbabwe and produce an exhibition of photographs of 'life in an ordinary African city.' My objective was to try and show people where the music they enjoyed came from. I chose Harare in Zimbabwe, as the Bhundu Boys, with whom I had become friends, were able to facilitate contacts and photo opportunities. The exhibition was shown in conjunction with the festival. The venue I chose was Eldon Square Leisure Centre where I reckoned it would be seen by the most people.

Rik Walton

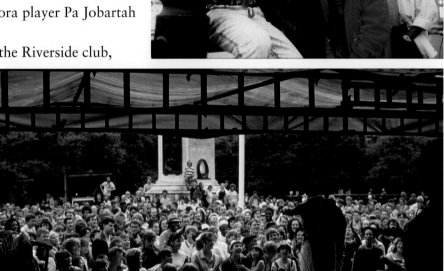

Top, the Bhundu Boys; above, Amayenga play at Old Eldon Square

Rik Walton

135

SCENES FROM CULTURE CITY

Clockwise from above, Baltic Mill, mid-1980s, before 'art' was heard of on the Quayside. Barbara Woodhouse, 1982, Eldon Square; The Light Programme, Northumberland Street, 1985; community art, back Chester Street, 1982.

But we did have fun!

Peter Thomson

May Day, 1988. The 'Jobs not Bombs' lorry leaves Ellison Place.

After a failure by the Labour Government of the late 1970s to come to terms with changes in Britain and the wider western world, Thatcher's Conservative government came to power in 1979 with a very different agenda. For a number of Tyneside-based performers, artists and political/community activists, this was a period of intense creative activity with a very different approach to cultural engagement. It embraced the basic principles of socialism in the Labour movement but opposed much of its practice.

We're talking fun here: politics as fun? What? A new approach to socialism – a cultural approach, asking what kind of a world do we want to create?

One of the most significant cultural changes was the challenge to male domination. Take the annual May Day March, an event steeped in tradition that began to attract less conventional political activists. For example, lesbian feminists joined the march each year under a banner proclaiming 'Lesbian Liberation' – to the discomfort of some trades unionists who accidentally found themselves marching behind it!

There was a group of very active feminists organising women-only events and women-only campaigns, based around the Women's Centre in Pink Lane, which also incorporated the Tyneside Rape Crisis Centre. Management committees (or, more accurately, collectives) were established, workers were employed, and the Centre hosted a number of women's groups as well as social events. When Newcastle Lesbian Line was founded it was hosted by the Women's Centre. Having space in the Centre meant that essentially the Line only needed sufficient funds to pay the phone bill, and a weekly women-only disco was sufficient to keep things going. Everyone had so many political commitments that when Lesbian

Line was set up, the collective met on a Friday evening because it was the only evening of the week that none of the members had other meetings to attend. Tyneside Rape Crisis Centre continues to this day as one of the longest running Rape Crisis Centres in the country.

And there WAS fun. Friggin' Little Bits was a low-tech, Newcastle-based harmony group who dared to not only challenge stigmatisation of lesbians but also to laugh at it. At a time when lesbian mothers were still losing custody of their children, just because they were lesbians, and when the government started to talk about lesbian families as 'pretend families', the Friggin Little Bits was hugely important in asserting the right to be a lesbian, and be happy and proud.

Other groups were creating alternative resources such as the Tyne and Wear Resources Centre, Law

Poet and activist Julia Darling fronts an International Women's Day march, St Mary's Place, 1982.

Centres in both Newcastle and Gateshead, Children's Warehouse, and a host of community-based and community-focussed arts and cultural projects and initiatives. All of these were, more or less, targeted at non-traditional audiences or groups who were generally excluded from participation in and consumption of culture as it had been traditionally defined. They soon spread throughout the region.

What did seem to explode at this time was the number of 'alternative' artists, particularly performers, who became based on Tyneside. Around the turn of the decade there was a proliferation of alternative or community theatre companies in and around Tyne and Wear including Wearabout, Bruvvers, Live Theatre, Mad Bongo, Skin and Bones, Puppets and People, Road Gang, Major Diversion, Change Gang, Quondam, Tyne and Wear Theatre in Education, Dodgy Clutch, NE1. This period saw the expansion of community arts projects. Uncle Ernie's Roadshow in Whitley Bay was soon followed by the Byker Arts Workers, Sunderland Community Arts, Them Wifies, Tyneside Community Music Project and many more.

Artists had gathered in and around the area creating a dynamic atmosphere. Spectro Arts and Children's Warehouse, just off Pilgrim Street, buzzed. Down on the Quayside the Amber Film and Photography Collective and the Side Gallery were becoming well established and soon to be world renowned.

The Red Umbrella Collective was brought together in 1980 by performers and musicians with a broadly feminist, green and socialist outlook, to encourage

Peter Thomson

Members of the Red Umbrella Collective shelter beneath their suitably large brolly on a march through Shieldfield, November 1981.

music, poetry and theatre to be interwoven in a political context.

One of Red Umbrella's first major initiatives was to create a street band to take part in Mayday celebrations in 1980. There was a strong non-militaristic ethos among participants so when it came to naming the band, they baulked at calling themselves a marching band, and became the Stumbling Band, open to any aspiring musicians. At least a dozen people took up an instrument in order to take part over the seven or eight years of the band's existence. The band saw itself as a resource to support a range of campaigns; from Anti-Apartheid to Trade Union demonstrations (and unofficial disputes too) to anti-nuclear events to anti-racism events. During the Miners' Strike of 84-5, they could be found most Saturdays at the Monument, raising money, morale and support.

Regular events were often introduced with the words: 'Welcome to another evening with Red Umbrella – a loose collective of radical performers – or is it – as

Peter Thomson

The Stumbling Band perform in support of Health Workers, Eldon Square.

CHRISTMAS DANCE
for PEACE
CHILDREN WELCOME
LATIN AMERICAN FOOD
REAL ALE
LATE BAR
SPECIAL EFFECTS
AND SOCIALISM
at: THE GUILDHALL
NEWCASTLE 16th DEC
FRIDAY 8:00 TIL LATE
THE BIG BAND, 30's & 40's MUSIC
THE LEGENDARY..PEANUTS
DANCE BAND   RED MUSIC
ALL PROCEEDS TO NEWCASTLE TRADES COUNCIL
TICKETS UNWAGED £1:20 FROM DAYS OF HOPE BOOKSHOP and
WAGED £2:40   THE PEOPLES BOOKSHOP
WESTGATE RD.

Peter Thomson

some would have it a radical collective of loose performers. You, the audience, must decide!'

At one time the Mayday Dance and the Christmas Dance for Peace and Socialism were events attracting hundreds of people, filling the Guildhall on the Quayside to bursting point. Here are some names that might stir a memory or two: Sugar and Spikes, We Don't Want The Peanuts We Want The Plantation Dance Band, Ongoing Situation, The Rock and Roll Rescue Band, Red Music, Street Abuse, The Old Rope String Band, The Poetry Virgins, The Country Picket, Burning Brass, The Bakelite Band, Wireless Wireless, Barking Iron, Hidden Talons, Women May, Tyneside Community Choir, The Rescue Band, The Brighton Palais Orchestra, The Law and Order Band.

Peter Brabban

A benefit for the miners, Guildhall, 1984.

The power of culture to change lives was embraced and celebrated. After 30 years it is satisfying to see how well creative artists on Tyneside perceived the new politics that were emerging, and how their celebration of the new offered up different ways of interpreting the world, even though those expressions were belittled, marginalised and ignored at the time. In the wider world the greed of the new 'me, me, me' politics took a powerful hold. The 1980s was the decade of the yuppie, the earliest mobile phones and the 'fill yer boots' culture engendered by the deregulation of the City of London. For 20 years the values of community, of collective strength, of support for the marginalised and excluded, and the importance of Britain's industrial base, were systematically demonised and trashed in favour of individual aspiration and what we now know to be the irresponsible gambling of financial engineering. Building wealth as solid as a house of cards.

In the true spirit of the 80s this piece was cobbled together in a collective fashion by
Caroline Airs – Jim Fowler – Ellen Phethean – Peter Thomson – Helen Walker

Multi-Culture

I was a member of the Multi-Cultural Arts Group, which was based at the old Todd's Nook School. I worked on quilts, candle making, leather jewellery, batik and embroidery. There were many workshops that we could take advantage of and we even had a dark room to develop our own photographs. We made cards, cushions, pictures and calendars as well as wall hangings for International Women's Day. The MCAG was renamed Chandni which means moonlight and it survived into the 1990s. It was a wonderful group and I learned so much.

Yvonne Young

Yvonne Young

Chandni celebrating International Women's Day in 1992.

Viz-ual culture

M y career as a creator of some of the world's favourite foulmouthed cartoon characters began at the twilight of the 1970s among the musicians, poets and artists of post-punk Newcastle. At the door of the Gosforth Hotel's function room on Gosforth High Street, my brother Chris and I and our school friend Jim Brownlow sold our rather amateurish 12-page black-and-white comic to the largely underage crowd that frequented the sweaty and noisy Monday nights.

As the 1980s began I found myself, age 15, at the centre of the most exciting cultural explosion. The ethic of the post punk world was driven by the idea that everything was rough, pared down and independently produced. The co-operative nature of this movement was genuinely supportive, everybody helping everybody else to promote anything the new generation had to offer. In a city that was gripped by a deep recession, this artistic oasis was a saviour to those of us facing a life of seemingly little prospect. I left Heaton School in the summer of 1980 at 16, both insecure and rebellious. One might say with hindsight that this was a perfect combination for an artist.

Of course the music scene didn't judge anybody by their academic failings, I was accepted by the open-minded and cosmopolitan (for Newcastle at the time) mix of people who made up the bands playing those cherished Monday night gigs. They all seemed to like my work, and we three rather socially awkward young lads became part of the scene. Not long into the New Year the landlord of the Gosforth Hotel barred the Anti-Pop Monday nights, but soon Arthur 2 Stroke took up a Monday residency at

The Baltic Wine Cellar was just round the corner from the dingy Quayside, on Broad Chare. This photo was taken in 1981.

Right, George, gentleman of the road.

the Cooperage and the music scene found a new home on the Quayside, then a dark, rundown area of decaying industrial buildings, ancient shipping offices caked in pigeon shit, almost deserted but for a handful of Russian sailors, prostitutes and has-been gangsters. We three '*Viz* boys' began to drink with the musicians in a dingy and long-unloved pub called the Baltic Wine Cellar on Broad Chare. It was frequented by a sparse mix of dodgy-looking older people and a rather charming gentleman of the road called George, well-known and

143

well remembered by anybody who drank around the Quayside in the 1980s. *Viz* in those early days was our hobby, and a loss-making exercise; we did it for fun.

Often on signing-on Thursday, Chris and I would make our way to the Market Lane pub for sausage and chips, costing 80p. Occasionally we would go to the Post Office Inn opposite St Nicholas Cathedral, where we two would be half of the customers. The Post Office Inn had a brand new Flash Gordon themed pinball machine that would occasionally break the silence of this peaceful old-fashioned room by announcing in a loud electronic voice, 'Emperor Ming awaits!' followed a few minutes later by the equally unexpected, 'Try again Earthling!'.

Around this time I developed my love of greasy spoon cafés, my favourite being the Exo Café Bar on Clayton Street. We'd always take a break there when working on *Viz* at the Tyneside Free Press workshop, around the corner in Charlotte Square. This fabulous formica, linoleum and ceramic-tiled establishment had clearly seen better days, but still had some of that colourful post-war optimism in its fabric. There was also a café at the top of Northumberland Street which was seemingly open 24 hours. Chris and I would occasionally work all through the night in a bid to complete the latest issue of the comic, and then treat ourselves at around five or six in the morning with a walk to this little gem. The First Stop café inside the Eldon Square bus concourse, was good too, and my friend Paul Smith and I

would spend entire afternoons in there in the last few months of our schooldays.

In September 1981 I started as a part-time student at Newcastle College of Arts and Technology. I studied for my Art A-level at the wonderful old Bath Lane building. The overzealous lady who enrolled me also persuaded me to sign up for two O-levels at the Parsons Building, just off

The Free Trade, 1985. Just one of the many Viz-selling pubs.

The ads were hilarious. This one is from Viz in 1985. The advertiser was at the mercy of the Viz lads. And it worked!

Scotswood Road. I adored the Bath Lane building, I would have loved to stay there and become a full-time art student, but I was rejected. I was to pass my art A-level there in just one year, despite it officially being a two-year course, but, not surprisingly, I failed both of the academic O-levels miserably.

The comic went from strength to strength, and the pubs of Newcastle became both an integral part of our social lives, and an essential part of the *Viz* network. The mid-80s was to see *Viz* being sold over-the-counter in many of the city's most popular bars. Often a pool table would be the driving force behind a pub becoming our latest drinking hole, the Baltic Wine Cellar had one, but it was done up around 1982, becoming the Baltic Tavern, a far less characterful and much bigger establishment. The Royal Archer on Archbold Terrace in Jesmond was close to home for Chris and me; at one time it had three pool tables and for some time we both played on the pub's pool team. Two pubs were to become firm favourites, the Strawberry by St James Park, with its bare floorboards, free jukebox and of course pool table, and the Trent House, with its rather more cosy pool room upstairs. The manager of the Trent

House was Tom Caulker, who would go on to be a huge innovator in the Newcastle club scene. It was his idea to sell copies of *Viz* in the pub and before long the Egypt Cottage on City Road, the Free Trade Inn in Byker, the Barley Mow on Sandhill and the Strawberry followed. *Viz* was now on sale in the students' union shops, Volume Records and Pet Sounds, and major retailers Virgin Records and HMV. Possibly the kingpin in our popular success amongst teenagers lay in the support of Brian Sandals of the Handyside Arcade's Kard Bar, major retailer of posters, patches, badges, second-hand records and general tat to the teenagers of Tyneside since time immemorial.

Viz was now everywhere in Newcastle that was trendy. As the second half of the 1980s began I found myself off the dole and in profit. I began to reap the rewards of being young and successful through a product that put me at the heart of Newcastle's vibrant scene. Nights out would be spent in the pubs followed by the early hours on Tuesdays and Thursdays in Rockshots, where Tommy Caulker DJ'd.

Despite the 1980s being effectively a cultural desert for music, Newcastle at this time had some great live venues, including the short-lived but wonderful Dingwalls on Waterloo Street, in which I witnessed some great shows including Martha Reeves and the Vandellas. There was of course Riverside and the bigger venues to see major touring bands, Tiffanys and the Mayfair in particular. In 1981 I was turned away from the door of the Mayfair, after arriving with my ticket to see Slade. The bouncers told me that I wouldn't be allowed in because I was a skinhead. I didn't see myself as a skinhead, but the bouncer casually pointed to my ex-army combat jacket and Doctor Martens and said, 'You've got the hair, you've got the jacket, you've got the boots.' I attempted in vain to explain that Slade had been a skinhead band originally, how could they expect to turn away all the skinheads that want to see them? Not surprisingly, this was in vain, I walked away dejected, having sold my ticket at a profit. I'd wanted to see Slade since I was about six. I never did get to see them.

Simon Donald

Simon, with skinhead hair, in the Fighting Cocks.

COMIC Viz

More fun than a balloon and a large ice cream

YUMMY

Britain's foremost top number one premier leading magazine

Viz was gestated during my teenage years in the 1970s but it grew up and reached adulthood in 1980s Newcastle.

The shadowy Anti-Pop organisation put on gigs at the Gosforth Hotel on Monday nights when two punk bands alternately topped the bill – a weird three-piece called Arthur 2 Stroke and the more punchy Noise Toys. It all seemed very exciting compared to the rock and jazz bands that played in most pubs and the audience was very young, a large proportion of them being posh girls from Gosforth High. They were one of the main attractions. Andy Pop and Arthur 2 Stroke were the brains behind Anti-Pop. They had an office at 20 Bigg Market. Me and my school mate Jim Brownlow went to see them, and asked if we could sell magazines at their gigs. *Viz* was launched in November 1979 at an Arthur 2 Stroke gig. Myself, Jim and my brother Simon sold copies on the door for 20p each. They'd cost about 40p each to print but people still complained about the price. The Beano only cost 6p.

In 1980 Arthur 2 Stroke's band got a residency at the Cooperage down on the Quayside. Me and Jim had started exploring pubs on the periphery of the city centre – the Bigg Market was too rough for a weedy Jesmond lad like me. The run-down Baltic Tavern on Broad Chare became my favourite haunt. Anti-Pop ran a rehearsal room round the corner and the pub buzzed with an eclectic mixture of musicians, actors (from the nearby Live Theatre), sailors and market traders.

Around 1982 the Baltic closed for refurbishment and the bohemians were dispersed like rats to other bars. The Quayside was being developed up, and all over town pricey wine bars were starting to replace the genuine, old-fashioned boozers. I fled to the Trent House, which was a bit of a student bar, but it had a brilliant juke box and a pool table, the two essential ingredients. Regulars there included local pop stars of the day like the Kane Gang. The Strawberry was also on my drinking circuit. Like the Trent it was an old, run-down pub, rejuvenated by a canny landlord and with lively bar staff.

Traditionally for after-hours entertainment I'd head for the Poly or University student unions, and beg to be signed in by a passing student. It annoyed me that students had so much provided for them and us townies were second-class citizens. For a while the Jewish Mother was the place to go when the pubs closed. You paid £1.50 to get in and the admission fee included a burger and chips. You rarely saw the burger and chips but that didn't matter.

The Jewish Mother gets busy, from The Crack, 1989.

I'd worked at the 'Ministry' after leaving school and I was accepted by my clerical working class colleagues as one of the lads. We went to see strippers at the Hofbrauhaus in Waterloo Street, and went to the mainstream nightclubs, like In Cognito in the Cloth Market, and Madisons by the Centre Hotel. I left the DHSS to go full-time as a self-employed graphic designer in 1981.

I worked for all sorts of people. The Mayfair, Northern Arts, record labels, music promoters, clothes shops. Meanwhile I was publishing *Viz* in my spare time, and selling it myself in pubs, at gigs and in the student union bars. The first shop to sell *Viz* was Volume Records in Ridley Place, then the Kard Bar in Handyside Arcade. Brian Sandalls, the Kard Bar's owner, provided me with lots of business advice. I was quite blasé about it, producing a comic whenever I felt like it, but Brian would hassle me and keep asking for a new issue. Sales of *Viz* first took off there.

The city centre was always evolving. For me the halcyon days were 1980 to 1984. The Hofbrauhaus closed down and became Dingwalls, part of a national chain of small music clubs. I designed a lot of their promotional material for them and saw some great bands there. But it went bust, then re-opened as The Bear Pit. That didn't work either. Then Paul Cannell, an ex-footballer got involved, and it became Zoots, aimed more at the mainstream, CIU club type audience. I think that was Newcastle's problem in terms of music culture. The guy who had the Trent House also ran the Barley Mow on the Milk Market down by the Quayside. That became very trendy, but the crowd there always seemed a bit darker, and gothy. The Egypt Cottage was another bar on the circuit. Next door Tyne Tees TV was producing *The Tube*, and it wasn't unusual for world-famous pop stars to wander into the bars on a Thursday or Friday night. If you wanted a quiet drink with no danger of Spandau Ballet walking into the bar you could always go to the Free Trade, a cracking pub overlooking the river in Byker.

Viz was signed up in 1985 by Virgin Books. I was surprised when the humour translated, first from students and punks to Geordie people in Newcastle, then from

Simon, left, in pink hanky, and Chris Donald celebrate Viz's success in the Egypt Cottage.

Geordies to people all over the country. *Viz* sales reached a million, and I became a father in 1989. I didn't got out much after that. Generally speaking, I disapproved of the way the city centre leisure industry went 'up market' in the eighties. I hated the cocktails, the padded shoulders and the stupid haircuts. But if you had your wits about you and your ear to the ground, there was always somewhere to go, something happening.

Chris Donald

Newcastle on film

Mike Figgis's film *Stormy Monday* was shot on location in and around Newcastle during the early summer of 1987 and released the following year. This moody, darkly atmospheric crime thriller follows Finney (Sting), the owner of a seedy quayside jazz club, as he fights off a crooked American property developer, Cosmo (Tommy Lee Jones).

The Tyneside of the 1980s we see in this film combines a vanishing industrial past with the emergent service economy that was attempting to replace it. Gone are the spit-and-sawdust pubs of yesteryear, replaced by the champagne and white tablecloths in the wine bars of Dean Street. The derelict Baltic flour mill stands by an almost deserted river, with only the *Tuxedo Princess* moored beneath the Tyne Bridge to keep it company. The buses – still painted yellow – sail past distant shipyard cranes, but it's the Metro that Brendan (Sean Bean) uses to make his way across town. The Royal Station Hotel is the swankiest venue in the city and it costs 'fifty pounds a night' for Kate (Melanie Griffith) to stay there.

Only a decade after the fall of T. Dan Smith, the whiff of local political corruption still lurks just below the surface, represented amongst the minor characters in the shape of a bent city councillor. One telling assessment of the region's contemporary economic status emerges when Cosmo makes a speech at a civic banquet in the Assembly Rooms, remarking in the recognisably Thatcherite vocabulary of the time that: '… in this once great area the going is tough, so it's time the tough got going' and that the city needed 'major surgery'.

Many scenes and aspects of the plot are reminiscent of, if not an actual homage to, an earlier Geordie classic, *Get Carter* (1971). The familiar trope of cockney gangsters coming north and getting more than they bargained for is reflected when two of Cosmo's London henchmen are sent packing on the train back south, bloody and broken-boned. Finney and Cosmo hold a meeting in the Victorian-noir setting of the pedestrian walkway on the High Level Bridge. Another reminder comes when a street parade of New Orleans jazz bands and majorettes making its way down The Side (it's 'America Week' in the Toon!) is followed by a local juvenile jazz band of the type Jack Carter had seen the previous decade.

Strutting in front of these baton-twirlers is a bowler-hatted Master of Ceremonies played by local actor Harry Herring. One other on-screen face that would have been very familiar to many Newcastle residents is that of a newspaper seller played by Jimmy Forsyth – better known as a photographer and chronicler of day-to-day life on the Scotswood Road of the 1950s and 1960s.

Though a fine film, there isn't a lot of regional flavour to *Stormy Monday*. Newcastle serves more as a representational backdrop for a generic northern town, its distinct character even further diluted by the 'America Week' of the plot. Nonetheless, this movie would help pave the way for Tyneside's cultural rebirth on the small screen over the subsequent decade. The TV series *Finney* (1994) took the form of a prequel, following the eponymous jazz club owner's life in the years before *Stormy Monday* was set. This show, along with others such as *Spender*, *55 Degrees North*, and *Crocodile Shoes*, would help to make Geordie accents a familiar and well-loved sound in the nation's living rooms.

Christopher Goulding

Carol Macdonald

What a hoot! I was an extra on the film *Stormy Monday*. Mike Figgis, the director, had a hell of a time trying to stop us giving the musicians in the film vodka. After being paid our wages for the week, we all trooped off to the favourite bar of the time, Berlin's down by Central Station, and partied till the early hours.

Carol Macdonald

A cracking mag!

I worked for Shaun Wilson and Ray Callan, who ran an entertainment business from an office on the Quayside in the mid-eighties. They promoted gigs at Tiffanys featuring artistes such as Nick Cave and Aswad, as well as a regular 'alternative' night in the club's function room, Mr M's. Every Friday I was given a pile of leaflets advertising their events to distribute in the pubs that I frequented of a weekend.

Leafleting – nobody used the term 'flyers' back then – was a cost-effective way of reaching a market, and many other businesses and club operators relied on it to drum up trade. By the evening's end, the tables and floors of pubs were festooned with drink-sodden sheets of paper, so the practice wasn't too popular with landlords and their punters. I came up with a solution that suited all parties.

Knowing how much it cost to print a thousand A5 leaflets, I approached the main litter merchants and suggested they gave the money to me instead. In return, their leaflet would become an advertisement in a similar sized magazine, which people would take home to read, rather than throwing on the floor. I'd also write a little about their event or venture, as well as a roundup of what was happening in the pubs, clubs and restaurants where it was distributed.

The old Tyneside term 'crack', meaning gossip or news, summed up the editorial content perfectly, so the magazine's name pretty much chose itself. In December 1985 *The Crack* was born: Newcastle's first independent free magazine serving the city's 'alternative' culture. A mate of Shaun and Ray's did the printing for a few beers, but thousands of copies had to be folded, stapled and distributed by me, as there was no money to pay for assistance. The whole operation was similarly low-tech.

My bedsit in Jesmond was so small there wasn't space for a table. I'd write the entire content of the magazine on an old typewriter on the floor – always the night before it went to press, the creative flurry helped and hampered by a combination of blind panic and several cans of Special Brew. A magazine would eventually

Marshall Hall

emerge from the sprawl of Cow Gum tins, scalpels, ink bottles, rulers, set squares and sheets of Letraset – a process that became redundant within a couple of years, when it could be knocked up with a lot less hassle on a desktop computer. Assuming, of course, you had space in your room for a desk.

The advertisements in the early issues provide a good snapshot of the times. There are several long-gone clothes shops, such as Retro Chic, in the Handyside Arcade, which sold tuxedos, trilby and top hats and antiques, and a shop called Clap on Old Eldon Square that had similar wares. For more contemporary punky stuff there was Phaze, on High Bridge. Volume and Old Hitz sold the most important music of that decade. Readers were encouraged to get their hair spruced up at 3D and Tiger Blue, and persuaded to let it down at restaurants such as Melbourne Diner, Jewish Mother and Heartbreak Soup.

All my favourite pubs advertised in *The Crack*, which was more than just a happy coincidence. The Bigg Market was beginning to take off and the city centre became an unwelcoming place for the arty, studenty, bohemian, or simply 'different' types, who did their drinking in bars on the periphery. I didn't want to waste my magazines on the sort of people who moved their lips when reading, so it was aimed squarely at the smart set, on a circuit I was well familiar with.

On publication day I'd load up a supermarket trolley with magazines and push it off to the Trent House. Tom Caulker took an ad in every issue and once payment had been received and part-spent on a drink, it was off for the same at the Broken Doll; maybe risking a visit to the Strawberry en route, depending on what I'd written about them that month. From the Doll it was downhill to the Barley Mow and Riverside then along to the Egypt Cottage, putting the magazines on tables, having a drink with the management, and picking up bits of drunken tittle-tattle for the next issue. By the time I headed off for the last drop at the Free Trade, I was

153

often being pushed in the trolley myself.

The Crack back then belonged to the fanzine era when editors prided themselves on the shabbiness of their product, and as such it was shining example. But desktop publishing made it easier to produce slick magazines, and people with far better business brains than mine entered the market. Davey Bruce started *Paint It Red* shortly after *The Crack*, using the first word processor I'd ever seen. As the decade progressed, *Coming Next* and *Monitor* looked as though they were produced by people who could actually use these machines, and Jim Mawdsley's *Boiling Point* was a dazzling triumph of the Apple Macintosh over the bedsit floor.

At one point there were half a dozen free magazines in Newcastle, each with circulations of several thousand. So I invested in some proper equipment in order to compete, and by 1989 *The Crack* looked almost normal (right). But I'm proud to say the content still lived up to its original strapline: 'a roundup of crack, rumour, gossip and the occasional downright lie'. I've had nothing to do with it for many years but it's also the only one of these magazines to survive, although admittedly not in the same spirit as the eighties.

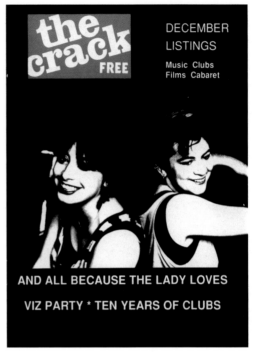

Marshall Hall

Marshall Hall

Razz-Razz-Razzmatazz!

Tyne Tees Television was thriving in the 80s, due to the huge amount of income from advertising revenue. ITV was the only TV company in the UK where commercials could be placed, so the advertisers paid whatever was required to get the best slots.

The Children's Department at Tyne Tees was particularly active, led by the inspirational late, great Andrea Wonfor, and we were making all types of programmes that aired nationally on Children's ITV – dramas like *Supergran*, factual programmes like *Madabout* with Matthew Kelly, and music programmes like *Razzmatazz*. This specialist knowledge and experience led to the commission of *The Tube*.

Lesley Oakden

I worked on the first three series of *Razzmatazz* (1981-1987) with Alastair Pirrie. It was a national kids' pop programme geared to young teenagers and went out at teatime having been recorded in chunks as live TV. There was no autocue and I remember executive producer Andrea Wonfor asking me to put together a two-minute review about a new pop book, which was a substantial piece to memorise. I did it, but then Andrea decided it was too long it needed to be edited down. When she saw my face pale, she said oh don't worry, just take it off the autocue … 'But', I said, 'there is no autocue!' It would have made the cameras too heavy and they had to zip in and out of the audience and not knock the kids' heads off.

Sometimes we went off and filmed inserts for the show. One expedition was to go out in a canoe into the North Sea. Another time we had to climb into the top of the TTTV tower.

The production team used to transport kids up from theatre schools in London in order to guarantee that children near the camera would be real 'performers' but lots of local schools were used every week and I still have people coming up to me saying they had been kids in the *Razzmatazz* audience.

Lyn Spencer, presenter

I went on *Razzmatazz* several times. Once was with Status Quo in 1983, another time was with Toni Basil. As part of the show one child would have to read some sentences as quickly as possible to be able to open the Peggy Babcock treasure chest (it was known as 'Doing a Peggy Babcock'), but

Lyn, Alastair Pirrie, and Madness on the set of Razzmatazz.

thankfully it wasn't me. I was in the first year at Kenton Comprehensive and our class went to TTTV studios in City Road for the whole day as the recordings were made over and over again. I thought it would be just the once, but it wasn't! There was rehearsal after rehearsal. They played a song and you danced, and they would pick out the best dancers. I got on, but just at the side, dressed all in red. The third time I was on *Razzmatazz* was with Madness. We all got a t-shirt and had to take them in to school the next day to show everyone. They were like nighties!

I was also on *Sunday Sunday* with Gloria Hunniford. There's a film of us washing a car with sponges just off Condercum Road, on a grassy area, and then we had to go to Tyne Tees Studios, and we were filmed running down a set of stairs. And after that every Sunday morning there we were on TV washing that car and running down stairs!

Sharon Reeve

Lyn Spencer

When I was around 10, at Bolam Street Primary, a group of people came in to audition us for *How Dare You*. I didn't get picked, luckily, but I was in the audience with my brother. There was a section in the middle where we had to pretend to be shown around by a wacky guy called Clive Webb. There was a competition between two schools doing daft things, and if you did it wrong green gunge dropped from the ceiling on to you. The trophy was a wellington boot!

Lisa Webb

The Useful Guide …

In the late 1980s I went back to Tyne Tees TV to do continuity, which was where I had started in the 70s. Producer Annie Wood decided she wanted me for her new series 'A Useful Guide to …'. And that became the best thing I ever did. Annie knew just what she wanted and for two years we worked together on two five-minute programmes each week. We explored topics such as *The Useful Guide to* writing a will, fitness for the over 30s, childminding, dog training, buggies, first aid, self defence … you name it we did it … over 200 of them. We used anything of my own that we could to illustrate the guides, the baby, the dog, the nanny. Annie liked the fact that just before I came to do the filming, she knew I'd been getting kids off to school or nursery and that I'd probably just put a wash in!

I vividly remember *The Useful Guide to Climbing Walls*. We went to South Shields and were met at a keep-fit hall by a huge ex-army guy. He got us to go up into the rafters, and then he said 'I'm going to hook you all to me and we're going to swing right across the space!' I had done my assertiveness training so I firmly said, 'thanks for the opportunity to swing through the air but we'll pass on that!' He took no notice, just grabbed me, and threw me through the air and then did the same to Annie and Joanne, the researcher. The day after that we had to do the filming …

One programme was about camping … we went right up the coast; filming took all day, and then TTTV contacted us and said there was a problem with the camera we had, so nothing had been recorded. They then sent another camera up in a taxi while we waited and we had to do the whole thing again that evening. There was a lot of time and research dedicated to making a five-minute programme. You could write in for the *Useful Guide* fact sheet after each programme.

Lyn Spencer

Lyn Spencer

Radio star, TV personality

Paddy at the desk at Metro Radio.

One of my most vivid memories from the Metro Radio breakfast show was John Lennon's death on December 8, 1980. I heard the 5am news, and that morning's show became a tribute to John Lennon.

I was doing lots of outside appearances and met some interesting characters, such as Rod Hull and Emu (*above, right*). I got the full Emu treatment. And I did crazy things, like going into a lions' cage, as a stunt! The lion tamer said don't look them in the eyes as they don't like that … but it was hard not to. That was on the Town Moor at one of the circuses.

I also broadcast a junior reporter spot at the weekend, with kids who wanted to try their hand at being on the radio. We interviewed Musical Youth (*above*), Wayne Sleep and Kevin Keegan among others. We'd record it, edit it and put it out on Sunday morning.

I left Metro Radio to go to BBC TV, which was then still at the old Broadcasting House on New Bridge Street. I worked with Mike Neville and Tom Kilgour, giants of North East news, in a very happy atmosphere. The old BBC studio was very small. When the old Broadcasting House finally shut in 1988 there was a huge party though the radio side of the BBC had already moved to the Pink Palace on Barrack Road.

You worked on a self-operated desk so as well as reading to camera you had to control other things yourself such as bringing up slides. It was a hairy operation! There were quite a few mistakes in the first few programmes I did, and it was live so there was no going back. There were two buttons, one for the slide to play and a reset button, so if you pressed the wrong one by mistake in the middle of the bulletin all the slides went back to the beginning. That happened a couple of times. Even when we moved up to Fenham, for the first few years a lot of bulletins were on a self-op desk. I put a piece of blue tack on one of the faders so I knew that was the one to press as they were so close to each other. You couldn't look down to see what to press, unlike on radio!

Paddy McDee

NCJ / Mirrorpix

Top, BBC Studios, New Bridge Street, 1987.

Above, Tom Kilgour, Mike Neville, Wendy Gibson, BBC Newcastle, Barrack Road, 1988.

Newcastle's First Night of the Proms

In 1988 my husband George was diagnosed with cancer and given about 12 weeks to live. Fortunately his case was taken on by Professor Proctor at the RVI who diagnosed non-Hodgkin's Lymphoma, treatable with chemo, and George lived for a further 13 years. Professor Proctor's team needed money for their research into blood-related cancers so we decided to try to raise £10,000 for them.

One of George's good friends, top baritone singer Benjamin Luxon, invited us to the Last Night of the Proms at the Albert Hall in 1988 and we had a wonderful evening. That was when George decided to organise his own Newcastle's Last Night of the Proms with Ben as a singer. It was a brilliant idea to raise money for cancer research through music. Later, George asked Ben if he would help him to say 'thank you' to the research department by singing at a concert in Newcastle, and Ben agreed. We knew that concert would be a sell out!

One day George slipped out from his isolation room in the RVI and booked the City Hall. On the way back he unfortunately bumped into the wonderful Sister Lorna Renwick, who was in charge of Ward 8, and she lectured him on the cost of keeping him in isolation and free from germs. She did have a twinkle in her eyes when he told her what he had been doing.

We then had the marathon job of raising sponsorship, which took well over a year, and finding an orchestra, a conductor and a choir. Luckily we both worked in education in Newcastle and North Tyneside so we sought the help of the music advisors. Everything slowly took shape. We made new friends in industry and businesses and journalist David Whetstone helped with wonderful coverage of the Proms in *The Journal*. Local television also helped. We were very grateful to them all.

All this time George was going through more chemo and then underwent a bone marrow transplant in the summer of 1989. The concert work helped him to get through all the treatment. He started to write down his feelings about having cancer, which became his first book *Cancer is Only a Word*.

George decided to call the charity North East Promenaders Against Cancer. Ben had spoken to Janice Cairns, a soprano, originally from Ashington, who had been leading lady in his last opera. She said we couldn't have a North East Proms without her. Unfortunately she had a really bad fall in *Tosca* just before our first Proms and did not make it, but she did take part over the next 23 years.

We now had our singer, conductors Len Young and Richard Bloodworth, the Durham Sinfonia, the Newcastle Choral Society and Ryton Choral Society. The day of the concert began at 9am with friends, young people from the Duke of Edinburgh Award Scheme, and family helping to blow up hundreds of red, white and blue balloons, put flags on every seat, and set up the stage. We were very fortunate to have chosen the City Hall as our venue. Manager Peter Brennan and the box office staff were wonderful. The capacity of the hall was over 2,000; we were soon sold out and people kept coming all that day to see if there were any returns so we never stopped. The day culminated in a brilliant concert with wonderful singing, lots of audience participation, flag waving and clapping until your hands were sore. On that night we raised £25,000.

George and I went on stage to thank everyone and while he was speaking a lady from the audience joined us and thanked George for all his hard work. Then she turned to the audience and said 'would you like another Proms concert?' There was a huge roar of 'YES'. Ben said he would come again if George would organise another one. That was how the Newcastle Proms concerts began.

North East Promenaders Against Cancer is still going strong. With the help of all the volunteers, sponsors, supporters, runners, cyclists and fund raisers we have raised £1,350,000 over the last 24 years. The research at the RVI has helped many people with cancer here and all over the country. It is a wonderful tribute to the generosity of people in the North East.

Rosalynde Walker

(Read Cancer is Only a Word @ www.nepac.org.uk.)

Jim Appleby

George thanks the audience at the 1993 Proms.

WEST END GIRLS

Pet Shop Boys, 1986

Fashionistas

The 1980s was an exciting period for fashion. It was when Newcastle caught up with London and Manchester, and developed an interesting and expanding range of fashion outlets. At the centre of Newcastle's fashion identity was the Fashion Department at Newcastle Polytechnic. The Department had developed a strong profile from the 1960s onwards, but it was in the 1980s that it really made its name. Mary Bromley had helped steer the Design School, and Fashion in particular, to national prominence by this time, with many graduates being employed in London, and in prestigious jobs in Europe and further afield.

The annual Polytechnic Fashion Show was an important event on the Newcastle social calendar and tickets were much sought after. It attracted fashionistas from all over the country. Punk, Italian and Japanese fashion were major influences on student work in the period and the show helped to bring an awareness of new international fashion directions to the City. I remember the gasps from the audience when some spectacular

Jeff Banks opens Newcastle Fashion Centre, 1988.

example of post-punk fashion was unveiled and the lengthy applause at the end of each performance. Local TV and newspapers always covered the event at some length. I still have a couple of jackets, from those shows. The shoulders are very wide indeed, but the jackets are still stylish and wearable. They remind me of the energy and innovation that characterised the students' work in that interesting period in fashion and style.

The eighties are often referred to as 'The Designer Decade' and there were a number of other ways in which this was visible in Newcastle. New designer shops selling menswear opened around High Bridge, joining more established designer outlets in the City. At night the 'toon' seemed full of Don Johnson lookalikes, with jacket sleeves rolled up, highlighted hair, designer shirts and Polo aftershave wafting behind them as they paraded in the Bigg Market. Young Geordie men began to show

Warehouse, Blackett Street, 1988.

their more feminine side as they shopped for designer fashion as enthusiastically as their southern counterparts.

High-street outlets such as Next and Warehouse brought an affordable designer look to Newcastle. They were part of an expansion of national fashion chains that impacted significantly on the retail profile of regional cities. The Next department store opened at the foot of Northumberland Street in 1986. The interior was like a high end London designer shop, the kind of outlet to be found in Covent Garden or Knightsbridge. Its three floors incorporated a hairdresser, flower shop, interiors, café – as well as men's, women's and children's wear. George Davis, whose concept it was, was interested in Italian and Japanese fashion and that was picked up on in the early Next collections. Much of the menswear was Armani influenced, but highly affordable. Linen jackets with shoulder pads, as well as looser clothes in natural colours, were very much the early Next signature.

Next's department store opened on the site of the old Woolworth's in Spring 1986. In 1989 it moved further up and onto the opposite side of Northumberland Street.

Next was Newcastle's first brush with what was called 'lifestyle marketing'. You could buy your whole design identity in one place with the same retail signature. Other chains such as River Island and Benetton contributed to a broadening retail culture in the city and more established outlets were 'made over' to look more design conscious. Newcastle was very much involved in the massive development of fashion and design retailing in this country the 1980s, which transformed the look of the High Street. We 'shopped till we dropped' in Northumberland Street and beyond. It seemed like such fun at the time.

Hilary Fawcett

I went very blonde, nearly peroxide and had my hair cut shorter and layered at Wildes. Going out was big thing and clothes were very glam, with lots of different styles like new romantics and retro. If you wanted to look different you could wear a tuxedo jacket, or a bow tie, or a leather tie. Hats made a big comeback. I had a couple of toque hats, like little pill boxes that sat on the side of your head. I had a lovely dull gold/bronze trench coat made of quite heavy material, and I had a bronze toque, that went with it … understated! I had a cream coat, like a long mackintosh, and a black and cream toque that went with it. There were lots of hats in Fenwick's. That was early to mid 80s. The Dallas look came in during the mid to late 80s, when you started to get big shoulder pads. You rarely got a garment that didn't have some kind of a shoulder pad, even t-shirts and jumpers! The colours were very bright electric blues, pinks, vivid greens.

I liked Wallis, which had been around for a while but it came into its own and adapted catwalk fashions for the high street. Next was emerging as a front runner and had nice affordable fashion. Fenwick's as usual had great fashion, especially Fenwick's French. Also Marks and Spencer seemed to do very well and captured the market with their leather skirts and jackets. I had a lovely red leather skirt from there and a jacket in red suede with leather collar and cuffs. Warehouse opened too. There were some good individual boutiques like Cream on Hood Street that had designer clothes, and Leaf on Pilgrim Street. I became more sophisticated as I had more money to spend and I liked the clothes.

People used to get dressed up when they went out so I didn't seem out of place.

Kath Cassidy

Skirt and jacket from Wallis, 1988.

DIY dresses

Karen Laidler

My aunt and Nana had ballgowns from the 1950s which I customised. I also had my grandmother's Nottingham lace wedding dress and I would wear it with a leather jacket and Doc Martins. I wore the petticoat as a dress too. It ended up falling to bits.

Clothes were very individual. I ended up somehow with a leather jacket that had belonged to Menzies from the Angelic Upstarts. The lining was ripped out! We didn't want to copy anyone else, and I suppose we destroyed a lot of clothes. In the early 80s we customised lots of things to be different, but the style was softer than the 70s punks. I had a favourite trilby hat.

I bleached my hair, and by accident ended up brown at the back like Debbie Harry. The hair had to be as white as possible and even two bottles weren't enough for my long hair. The dyes were very harsh in those days. We probably ruined our hair.

I made a Debbie Harry style 'banana dress' for a 'banana and pomegranate' party. It was made from gorgeous old yellow curtains. I wasn't a good sewer, I just drew round myself with a felt pen and tacked it together. But I went out in that dress as it looked really good.

Some people wore ra-ra skirts in layers. Vivienne Westwood created the puffball skirt in the 80s. It looked like a lampshade, but it caught on. The shoulder pads were awful.

If you were just a 'normal' person, perms were the thing. Men might be short and spiky on top and long at the back. Kevin Keegan was very permed! It wasn't a very good style.

Karen Laidler

In 1986 my sister, Grace, asked me to be one of her bridesmaids. I was delighted but the only dresses we could find in shops were frilly and in pastel colours. As I didn't want to look like a meringue, there was only one thing for it – I would have to make my own dress. We found a pattern we liked and some mid blue moiré watermark silk taffeta. There were bows on the shoulders, just like Sarah Ferguson had on her wedding dress.

Angela Merritt (née Wong)

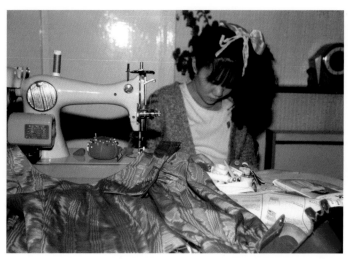

When I got married in 1986, I wanted all my friends plus my sister and two nieces to be my bridesmaids – yes eight bridesmaids! To help keep the costs down, my sister and I made all the bridesmaids dresses ourselves. All the girls shared the cost of the moiré taffeta bought from Fenwicks – I think it worked out about £20 per dress.

Hazel Hunter

My mam made great big baggy jumpers for me and I did my own designs on t-shirts with t-shirt paint. We did tie dying with black jeans and bleach and used those little dyes that you put in a bucket of water. I made a lot of things. My mam also knitted trendy half-and-half coloured jumpers. There were lots of second-hand things too. I bought checky shirts from Flip. I'd wear pyjama tops too and wore my denim jacket inside out! I never went to Fenwick's or places like that.

Paula Ginger

Flip advertises in Courier, 1983.

Proper Goths and other fashion victims

We got our clothes at Phaze on High Bridge, the Goth Mecca. We also went to Clap or Attic; it was quite difficult to get stuff we liked. These were early Goth days and we were proper Goths, and wore silver bracelets up our arms and lots of rings. We were serious, very cool … and hung out on old Eldon Square. We'd go to Pet Sounds, and then traipse up to Volume to see what they had, and to Old Hitz which was in one of the little portacabins behind the bus station on Percy Street. There was Pasha, and a comic shop, was it called Timeslip? There were odd little shops in Leazes Arcade, and a jewellery shop on Leazes Lane. Scorpio in the Green Market was the only place for Goth boots.

Kemi Kilburn

Phaze, photographed in 1995, and an advert from Viz, 1987.

The shop was a huge success and Phaze regularly appeared in Viz so the dodgy adverts were only an extra attraction.

C&A and Top Shop were my favourite haunts for clothes shopping in Newcastle. I had a long blue tube skirt, a long blue and white print blouse, a red belt to wear over the blouse and a string of tacky, red plastic beads all from C&A. I proudly wore that outfit to sit one of my O-levels. I have fond memories of my pink boob tube, my long gypsy skirt with the petticoat hanging below it, my fluorescent shoes and socks, my off-the-shoulder jumper, my leg-warmers and Fame sweatshirt combo and of course my ra-ra skirt. I'm sure my ra-ra skirt was the only one in the country that had an extra frill sewn onto the bottom. My Mum thought it was indecent otherwise, but I was mortified. I can clearly see the windows of the clothes shops along from the Green Market, inundated with Frankie Says t-shirts. I never got one of those either. Our school suffered from 'fashion' as well. Yes, we had to wear grey skirts and tights or socks. Nobody specified the length of the skirt. So what could they do when girls turned up wearing mini-skirts and over-the-knee socks, which had the added bonus of exposing inches of white flesh? The boys seemed to shuffle around in green Parkas with their hoods up though, so I doubt many of them noticed.

Kirsty Ferry

Sarah Hall

I owned red, pointy, boots with laces on the side and pastel coloured court shoes. I had a flying suit with a big collar and coloured polo shirts.

There was the Pod shoe shop, Ricci, near the Monument. I was desperate for a pair of Pods. They were all different colours, flat with a white sole, a T bar and a tag on the buckle.

Barbara Bravey, Sharon Reeve

Sarah Hall's pink ra-ra skirt (top) didn't suffer from an extra frill. Her suede shoes with acid yellow snakeskin were bought from Cruise, next to Rick's on the Cloth Market (where her parents bought her a Tequila Sunrise cocktail), and her plasticised skirt was bought in Phaze.

Shoulder pads or Laura Ashley?

When women were trying to smash through the glass ceiling in so many careers, they needed to project a big, powerful image, like a man. I think this was one reason why shoulder pads became so popular during the 1980s. TV programmes like *Dynasty* and *Dallas* played their part too.

Shoulder pads weren't without their problems. Once you'd put on a t-shirt with shoulder pads, a blouse with shoulder pads, a cardigan with shoulder pads and a coat with shoulder pads you looked like an American footballer. But we all had big hair that balanced out the massive shoulders.

You could go for the shoulder pads, the Flashdance look (footless tights, legwarmers and sweatbands) or the Madonna look (fishnets and pointy bras). Instead I embraced the 'Railway Children for grown-ups' look that was Laura Ashley.

I had a sailor dress (pink damask, worn with pink flat pointed shoes), a dark green corduroy coat with a frilled collar, tiered floral skirts and Edwardian-style high necked blouses with lace insets. I also had a pale blue flowered dress with a huge collar, which should have been worn by a pantomime milkmaid. On the other hand I had a beautiful oatmeal coloured fair isle sweater with a design of rose and crimson pansies. It cost £25 in the sale and took all my Christmas money.

The first Laura Ashley shop in Newcastle was in Nelson Street. With polished wood floors and shopfittings, rugs, pictures and furniture upholstered in Laura Ashley fabric, it was the epitome of style, and given the chance I'd have moved in like a shot.

Vanessa Histon

Heading for Laura Ashley, Nelson Street, 1982.
Inset, from North East Times, 1983.

In pursuit of that suit

Although I had amassed quite a collection of suits from second-hand and charity shops, I had never managed to find that one special suit. I had tried all the obvious places, but to no avail. I think the look I had in my head was from a picture of Billy Fury on the cover of one of my mum's old albums.

One place I often tried was Attic. This was on the third floor in a terrace of shops looking onto the Haymarket bus station. It was above a gent's hairdressers called Top Style, which specialised in helping men that were either bald or needed cover-ups. I definitely did not suffer from this affliction and I'm sure as I passed them on the staircase they would look at my golden locks with envious eyes … they may have thought I was just another punter, sporting one of the more expensive wigs on sale!

Attic was run by a lovely fellow and if you told him what you were after he would keep an eye open for you. I did get a wonderful navy blue Crombie coat from him, but never found my perfect suit at Attic.

From Viz, 1986.

So on to another of my favourite clothes shops, Fynd in Handyside Arcade. Although I did buy many items from Fynd, the holy grail of suits was not to be found here, though to be fair, I don't think suits were really their thing. I'm sure there was another clothes shop there, called The Little Shop. I got a couple of lovely collarless shirts here, the type that had button-holes to attach a separate collar.

If you went through the rear entrance of Handyside Arcade and crossed the road you would find another brilliant shop called Trash. No suits for me there, but a brilliant pair of black motorbike boots. I got the cobbler in Gosforth to sew some extra buckles and straps at the back and wore them with my bleached jeans (very Mad Max). Flip was another shop that I would often check out. Always plenty of suit jackets and trousers, but earlier fifties in style and not really what I was after.

Paul Merrit

And then it happened. I was walking along High Bridge in Newcastle and saw a clothes shop called Propaganda, which I had not seen before. I opened the door and there was a rack of suits that looked very late fifties/early sixties. The first one I picked up looked perfect, made of green shiny fabric with long thin lapels and side vents. I tried it on, but the problem was that it was far too big for me.

Thankfully my girlfriend Jenny was a genius with a sewing machine so I decided to take a chance and purchase the suit. It was £8, a bargain. I presented it to Jenny that evening and asked if she could do anything with it. 'Oh my God! Suits are really hard!' she said. 'Even a tailor would find this difficult.' But she measured me and said 'Leave it with me.' About two weeks later, when I had almost forgotten about it, she said 'Ok do you want to try it on?'

'You just try and stop me, Jenny'.

I put the suit on and I was amazed. She had cut about eight inches out of the back then sewn it back up, removed a huge amount of the material from each side of the trouser leg and tapered them. It was perfect. I would wear it with my black overcoat and a white scarf and Oxford shoes, which I had got from Fynd.

These truly were the best of times. A second-hand suit, second-hand coat and second-hand shoes and I felt like a million dollars.

The only give-away that I wasn't from the fifties, was I often wore a black ribbon on the end of a pig-tail at the back of my hair, which my girlfriend, Jenny would put in for me. I got the idea from the old black and white French TV production of *Robinson Crusoe* (the one with the lovely tune).

Paul Merrit

Shopping involved a Saturday walk around town where we always visited Marcus Price, Cruise and Ricci; they were probably the better shops at that time. Plus Four was popular for jeans and mid-priced stuff. We still had punks, the mod revival, new romantics and the casual football style coming in. Benetton Rugby tops in blue or green were very popular as were (horrible) pod shoes from Ricci. All the high-end sports brands were coveted by the casuals, including Lacoste shirts and Tacchini track tops.

Dale Toothill

By 1989 What Everyone Wants had opened on Newgate Street … not high end!

JOHN & SURTEES
Hair Base
28 Mosley Street
Newcastle upon Tyne
Tel: 612951

John Kelly

Hair dos

We opened John and Surtees Hairbase in Mosley Street on 16 June 1980. We had very little money, but we clubbed together and raised £4000 and did the shop up with various bits and pieces. We had green hessian for the walls, and we stripped the wood back to its natural colour. We were quite successful from the start. After the first or second year we hired a nightclub, Reflexions, for our Christmas party.

We'd worked in Brown's and similar places and been down to Sassoon's in London for courses. As we built the business up we tried to maintain a Sassoon influence. Popular haircuts at the beginning of 80s were layered, and we adapted them to our own methods and the Sassoon style. It involved a lot of precision cutting. Lots of women wanted to look like Lady Diana with her flicked back fringe.

There was a lot of perming, even for men. Men often had low lights in their hair. There were some outrageous hairstyles. Colouring was creative; we used henna and other natural colours. We mixed henna with coffee to get a darker colour and the red henna was very vibrant. We'd wrap hair in brown paper to get a different tone. The henna had lovely conditioning properties

Rival nearby establishment Sauvage advertised their styles in North East Times, May 1983.

Gary & Hilary

...have come from there, but Gary and his Sauvage team intend to make London sit up and take notice. Determined to make a name for themselves with their fresh and exciting outlook towards all aspects of hairdressing, they are already working on new ideas for 1984, which at the moment are of course a well kept secret.

HAIR BY

SAUVAGE

unmistakably different

28 PINK LANE, NEWCASTLE UPON TYNE.   Tel: 618822
(near ABC Cinema Westgate Road)

but the trend died out by the end of the 80s. Styles became softer and more natural as the decade went on, not so stark. We wanted to be different and specialise in good hair cutting. We tried to please the client, there was a lot of competition so they had to be happy or they'd just go somewhere else! We couldn't dictate how people wore their hair, though we tried not to let anyone look ridiculous!

John Kelly

Dressing in style with Marcus Price

99 Grey Street was at the entrance to the Central Arcade, next to Windows. The top end of Grey Street was always extremely busy as the Arcade was a way through to the stores in Market Street. We extended the Marcus Price shop as the premises next door became vacant and we had the greatest space to continue our womens' wear range alongside the menswear, all under one roof.

We refitted the whole store in light woods giving a minimalist look and a great background for the clothes. At the same time the packaging and paperwork were redesigned with a new logo. The typeface was from the 1930s but looked modern and when printed on brown manila bags was perfect. The logo was flexible enough to work in other ways, for example on the glass of the windows, where we used various colours to suit the seasons.

Inside the shop the upper floor was given over to men's shirts and knitwear, while the women's wear was on the lower floor alongside the remainder of the men's clothing – suits, jackets, trousers, jeans, casual jackets and accessories.

In the women's department we stocked a number of UK companies that were also highly regarded abroad, including Betty Jackson, Nicole Farhi, Ally Capellino and Hardwear Clothing

Marcus Price

Company. Foreign labels included Willi Wear from the US by Willi Smith, one of the first designers to base his fashion line on street wear. This range appealed to a variety of customers – the young manageress of Jigsaw bought the same jacket as an older lady architect. Then we had Newman of France and the massively successful Marc O'Polo too.

Wonderful accessories were provided by Georgina von Etzdorf, a UK company started by three students from Camberwell College of Art who became seriously good. We also sold great jewellery, the hottest by Monty Don being extremely glitzy and flash.

In the men's shop the cornerstones of the business were Nino Cerruti and Georgio Armani suits, casual wear, shirts and knitwear. We also stocked Henry Cottons, Valentino and CP clothing from Italy, together with Faconnable and Newman of France. On top of this there were a number of UK companies, Nicole Farhi and Hardwear Clothing again and the quite exceptional Paul Smith, who not only supplied us with

amazing clothes, but also designer gifts for him and her. Whenever I was working in London I always brought pieces back with me. There was the evening I bumped into a very good customer and on putting down my bag as we greeted I heard the awful tinkle of broken glass. It was two glass Alvar Aalto vases in very small pieces!! To complement these labels we also used Marc O'Polo and Paul and Shark from Italy, and not least the wonderful Issey Miyake whose shirts used fabrics that were state of the art at that time.

This was not only the most expensive clothing we had handled, but it had the strongest look both on the racks and when displayed, supporting our main idea which was to merchandise the shop as a whole, with an integrated theme running through each season.

And finally, to close out the eighties, we had another first in the town and it was Ralph Lauren Polo. This was the decade that saw the start of the designer label shops.

Marcus Price

Marcus Price

Paul Smith and Marcus Price staff.

Up Town Girls at Elle

The eighties were good for Elle – we had always designed and produced a few young evening dresses, especially for boarding school girls and university students. The larger stores didn't cater for this market, and the school proms explosion was yet to happen in the UK. We did a strapless dress called a Melissa, which was so perfect that it ran for years, short, long, ballet length, in silks, taffetas, satins, velvet bodice with crepe skirts, crepe de chine, chiffon and velvet and print cotton. We started to make a matching cotton bolero in the print cotton, which made it modest enough for weddings at the church and dressy enough to dance the night away at the reception.

At the beginning of the 1980s an innocent, suitable and naïve young girl caught the eye of Prince Charles. She was very photogenic, and soon she was constantly in the press. One of the finest photos showed her in a black low-cut dress by the Emanuels (who later

Graham Oliver

The Melissa dress.

designed her wedding dress). We were inspired by this 'outrageous dress' to design a strapless, frill top dress with separate puff sleeves and a full skirt, bulked out with net slips. We called it Diana.

We couldn't make enough of these young ball dresses and were soon discovered by the charity and hunt ball markets. It was such a pleasure to us to see these young girls' delight, when they tried on our dresses. They were 'just what they had dreamed of'.

A green silk puff sleeved dress in the press inspired another popular style, that we called Newby Priory (the first one went to a very smart wedding in Yorkshire at Newby Priory). The sleeves could be on the shoulders or off. We also designed a pretty, off-the-shoulder-style, actually called a prom dress. Both of these styles were very popular with bridesmaids.

In truth these dresses we designed were inspired as much by Victorian styles as by the press frenzy of Diana-watching. Variations of our three most popular dresses can be seen in many Victorian fashion photos. The Sloane style, high necked blouses were a staple of Edwardian style, and Ossie Clark was making the floppy, frilled collared styles favoured by Diana in the 60s (even for Mick Jagger!).

The young princess was at her most beautiful in a

Gone with the Wind. Elspeth, right, and friend Hélène Dolder, model the Diana and Glyndebourne dresses before the Heart Ball.

pale printed chiffon dress by Belville Sassoon. We designed a version in net with a lace trim that looked a lot less demure in black spot net and lace; we called it a Glyndebourne dress. I had a gold version that I wore to the Heart Ball one year. I went with my good friend Hélène, who was wearing a print cotton Diana dress. As we trotted across the car park at the Gosforth Park Hotel we heard some lads remark 'look at the state of them, its like bloody *Gone with the Wind*'!

We were there because we had been selling so many ball dresses that we felt we had to go and check out what everyone one else was wearing – and a good percentage of the frocks at this ball were Elle dresses, which made us quite proud of our Newcastle customers.

We did try to keep track of which dresses were going to which 'dos' but as we used so many different fabrics, colours and prints, there was not usually a problem!

Of course the styles were young and fun to wear, so we were wholesaling them all over the country. The stores were taking notice and Bainbridge's was one of the first to be aware of the market. No one else was producing similar styles, so they bought them from us. Another big selling point was that we had low production costs. The store appreciated the decent mark up and the customers appreciated the reasonable price and the fact they were fun and easy to wear. The net underpinnings were sold separately instead of being built in to the dress. So once purchased, the slip could easily be worn with the next dress.

We sold quite a few dresses in various colours as wedding dresses. One of our shop girls and friends, Bridget, wore a navy crepe de chine Diana dress with her bridesmaid Toni in a print chiffon version, and her young daughter, Gemma, in a navy crepe de chine Glyndebourne style. The wedding was at St George's church in Jesmond.

Elspeth's daughter, Polly, modelled the sumptuous Newby Priory dress one cold morning in 1987 at the entrance to the doomed Handyside Arcade.

We had one girl who rushed in to the shop mid-week, needing a dress for her wedding the following weekend! Her friend was making her red camellias (which were out of season) by taking the petals off

179

red roses and reassembling them to look like camellias. Although the flowers had taken so much planning, the dress had not! She was delighted to find a net and lace Glyndebourne style in exactly the right shade of red.

Obviously we were selling day clothes too, and continued to stock ethnic-style suits, jumpers, shirts and dresses by other designers including Museum, Mosquito, Sticky Fingers and later, East.

We were very lucky to stock jewellery by Newcastle designer, Dave Gibson, who traded as Quantum. We dealt with him for most of the 40 years we were in business.

Elspeth Rutter

Elspeth Rutter

Elspeth celebrates 21 years of Elle, 1987.

In October 1984 the student newspaper *Courier* included an article on a fashion show (*right*) featuring clothes by local designer Paul Shriek.

By the late 1980s Paul, who had had a best-selling concession in Top Shop had set up a shop on Dean Street. Sarah Hall remembered there was a light-up goose in the window (she bought a similar lamp from Shabbitat in the Bigg Market) and that the sales were excellent. She bought this signed cushion.

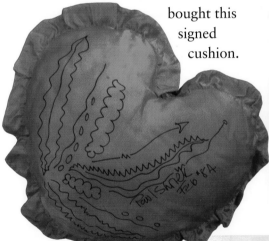

In 1987 the Edinburgh Fringe StopOver programme for Newcastle featured Paul Shriek.

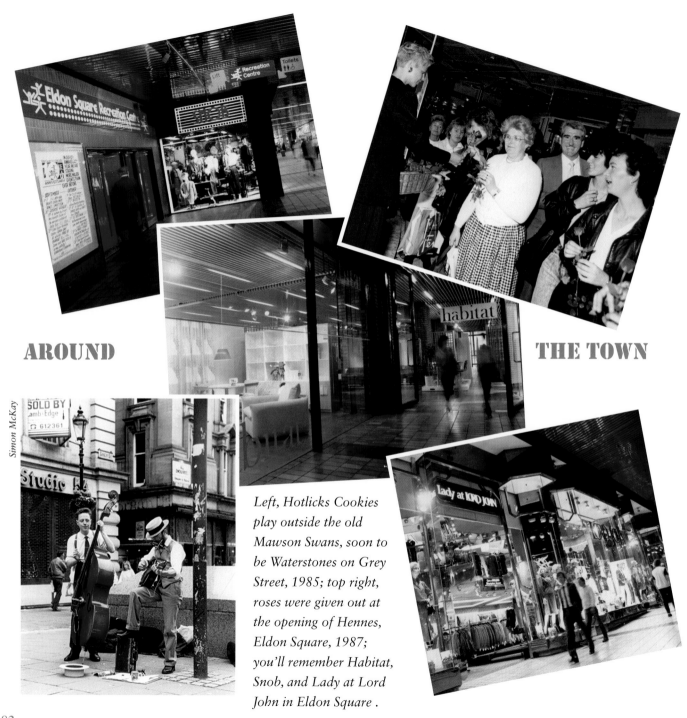

AROUND THE TOWN

Simon McKay

Left, Hotlicks Cookies play outside the old Mawson Swans, soon to be Waterstones on Grey Street, 1985; top right, roses were given out at the opening of Hennes, Eldon Square, 1987; you'll remember Habitat, Snob, and Lady at Lord John in Eldon Square .

Top left, the Royal Court pubs, off the Bigg Market, 1982; top right, Haymarket, 1989; far left; Princess Diana open the Findus Factory, 1983; above, a pristine Eldon Square, 1982; left, Café Procope advertises, 1987.

183

I STILL HAVEN'T FOUND
WHAT I'M LOOKING FOR

U2, 1987

Retail Therapy

I spent the beginning of the decade working for Derek Kirkup, who had several shops in the Handyside Arcade that traded under the name of Fynd. Derek was a collector of interesting, creative and exotic people, employing them in his hippie, punk and antique clothes shops, to develop a scene around the place. I was in a band and looking for some undemanding daytime work at the time. So I was happy to join his collection of oddballs and freaks, and ended up working there for three years.

The Arcade was a damp and shabby place in 1980, and hard to picture as the 'Carnaby Street of Newcastle' in its sixties heyday. But every Saturday it was a solid mass of long-haired teenagers – the forerunners of those on the Hippie Green a few years later – who spent the afternoons lounging around, chewing the fat, and doing some casual shoplifting. There was a regular culture shock at three o'clock on the dot, when a dozen skinheads would charge down the Arcade, windmilling their way through the wall of denim. Apart from that, their world was undisturbed.

Derek's empire catered for people of an 'alternative' bent, and his shops had an authentic enough whiff of the counter culture to make them 'hip'. The oldest one was Fynd Central, purveyors of bongs, chillums, scales, skins and other drug-taking paraphernalia to the region's 'heads' since the sixties. The reek of thousands of boxes of incense and several dozen Afghan coats was intoxicating in itself, and most of our weekend customers were school kids asking for 'Joyce sticks', 'hippie juice' and 'petunia oil', to recreate this heady atmosphere in their bedrooms.

The Afghan coats were the biggest money-spinners. They were bought for coppers and arrived direct from the country of origin, and us staff were issued with mallets to whack the maggots that spilled out when the crates were opened. The coats were shaken down, sprayed with some patchouli and put on a rail, with a price tag that was double my week's wages.

You'd think the arrival of punk would have buggered his profits, but Derek was over the moon when

Right, shop workers and shoppers enjoy themselves in Fynd, September 1981.

Above, the doomed Handyside Arcade in January 1987. This view is down the Gallowgate side of the horseshoe; Fynd was on the Haymarket side, but Hobo was a similar emporium. By the end of the summer the Arcade was empty and demolition followed to make way for a spanking new shopping arcade in the form of Eldon Garden. It was the end of an era.

it finally took off in Newcastle. In the early eighties he went down to the Kings Road to haggle with Malcolm McLaren and Vivienne Westwood over their latest designs (they would have been interesting encounters), but ended up finding a local sweatshop who could stitch lots of zips into reject trousers for a fraction of the price. We were soon selling hundreds of pairs of these bondage pants a week, at twenty quid a time.

Marshall Hall

Marshall Hall behind the counter at the Punk Shop, 1981. Nothing too demanding.

Come to think of it, every contemporary taste in fashion was catered for in the Arcade. Derek also had an antique clothing shop where punks, New Romantics and proto-Goths could find something fetching for a gig at the Mayfair, Uni or Poly, and an army shop which did a brisk trade in combat pants and paratrooper boots among an emerging movement of pale and intense men with brutal haircuts, whose musical tastes I could never fathom. John Woods' Frisco sold original American smart and casual wear, to people who were way more cool than any of us.

Everyday life in the Arcade was a hoot. Saturdays apart, all that was required of me was to open my shop at ten (the Punk Shop, or whichever outlet Derek thought I was best suited to that week) and stay awake until closing time. This was no great chore as he had assembled a fascinating set of colleagues, whose mates would hang out in the shops all day long. And there was Derek's inner circle of friends to entertain us. It was always a joy to see Moondancer strolling up the Arcade strumming his guitar, wearing nothing but his trademark purple velvet cloak and pink skimpy knickers.

By 1983 the writing was on the wall for The Arcade, there was talk of it being demolished and Derek began looking for other business opportunities. He opened a restaurant around the corner called the Barn, where he would collect ever more interesting and exotic people, and with redundancy looming I became a sales rep, selling Dobson's Fizz Bombs. But I didn't last long. It wasn't quite what my apprenticeship at Fynd had prepared me for.

Marshall Hall

Going, and gone. September 1987 saw Handyside Arcade desolate, boarded up and then demolished.

Top, the view from Percy Street.

Right, the view from the rear of the Arcade, a last glimpse of the glory that had gone.

May the force be with you

Crowds gathered on the pavement of Northumberland Street outside Fenwick's to watch the famous annual Christmas display. Parents pushed their excited children towards the plate glass windows. I thought I saw the huge figure of Santa on his richly loaded sleigh. You couldn't miss the seasonal music pulsating from large speakers. As magnificent as this Newcastle seasonal landmark was I had no time to stand and stare. I carried the heavy burden of serious business to attend to.

I was confident the toy department at Fenwick's would not let me down. This retail labyrinth had toys cunningly situated on the top floor. I remained focused as I made my ascent, careful not to become distracted by the huge range of goods on display. I hoped less

Fenwick's window, 17 December 1987.

disciplined consumers in search of the Millennium Falcon would fall for these marketing tricks.

Mid-journey, near an escalator, a wall clock caught my wife's eye. This could be a vital piece of equipment for the Pears' household, guaranteed to raise our social standing. I dismissed the thought, wise to focus on the business in hand.

On a cold winter day the sharp blast of warm air fired from overhead heaters as you enter the store is welcome. By the time you are on the top floor of the crowded store with your winter coat hanging loose, sweat pours. I felt in my pocket for my cheque book and cheque guarantee card as the slow moving escalator deposited me in the toy department. In early December there would surely be a huge selection of Star Wars toys and I was going to need them.

A weary sales representative scoffed when I asked if they had the Millennium Falcon in stock, perhaps a batch was waiting to be put out in display I suggested. There had been some, she had seen them, but parents who had timed their visit with inside information or sheer good luck had cleaned the stock out within hours. They had gone faster than the Millennium Falcon could cross the galaxy.

Panic set in. From the doors of Fenwick's I zigzagged Northumberland Street, avoiding the traffic, to Littlewoods, British Home Stores, C&A, Marks and Spencer. Nothing! There was no sign that Star Wars existed, no evidence of the most popular film of the era. Clearly rival parents had already conducted a raid.

Pushed to the back of Eldon Square was a shopping experience

Buses weave through the crowds on Northumberland Street, December 1987.

relatively new to Newcastle. I had inspected it before but rarely used it, now it might just be my saviour. It was called Argos. I had explained the concept to my father, who incredulously repeated the vital information to me 'So you go into a shop to look at a catalogue, queue to place an order, queue again to pay for it and they throw your stuff down a chute'. He had the gist. On this Christmas visit to Argos I only queued once to be told stocks of the Millennium Falcon had long since flown from the shelves.

I headed back towards Northumberland Street again performing a sweep of all the shops I could think of and discovered some I did not know existed. By the time I was in Wengers, at the bottom of Grainger Street, I knew I was defeated.

Just before Christmas day a work colleague informed me of a newsagent on West Road that was selling pukka Star Wars toys, I dropped everything to make an emergency dash to this unlikely destination. Inside the modestly-fronted shop was an impressive gathering of Star Wars figures and I bought a selection, all the ones I knew my son did not already have in his collection. Some I thought he did already have but they were wearing different clothes. They did not have the Millennium Falcon, but Christmas was not going to be a total disaster.

I held fast to my promise of purchase after Christmas. Thirty years on the Millennium Falcon is still in my loft. Together with an AT-AT (All Terrain Armoured Transport), TIE Fighter, X-wing fighter, Darth Vader's personal spaceship and a whole host of other spaceships and monsters cleverly marketed. As new merchandise was produced, I religiously bought every one. It was worth every penny.

Graham Pears

I loved Hamley's on Northumberland Street. I went for My Little Pony and Barbie dolls. And Care Bears. There were huge escalators going up. It was massive! I had Lights Alive and Etch a Sketch.

Kim Dryden

Northumberland Street, 1987.

arks and Spencer started to sell toiletries and make-up. The peach scented range of soaps, moisturisers, bubbles and deodorant was my favourite. Shower gels in upside down bottles appeared. The Bodyshop franchise came north and you could buy scents by the ml from a shelf full of apothecary style bottles.

Sarah Hall

Bodyshop, right, was spanking new in the Central Arcade in 1988.
Another new shopping experience was the Leazes Arcade which was converted from the old synagogue in 1984 and contained many little shops and cafés. It was severely damaged by fire in 1989 and only the external walls and cast iron beams remained. It was converted to student flats in 1994.

Shopping in Jesmond

Jesmond in the late 1980s was serviced by Wm Low supermarket. It sold Scottish bread, booze and pensioner foods, lots of meaty things in tins. The off licence was a large cage in the corner that had to be entered after your main shop was completed and was only open at certain times of the day.

The Acorn Road area had a post office, butcher and two greengrocers, 'Mangetout' and 'Haricot Vert'. Both had bargain bins where I would pick up cheap avocadoes. Manor House Road boasted the UK's (allegedly) most expensive corner shop that sold caraway bread and cocktail lemon slices, a junk shop, a launderette and a newsagents. Francesca's was always a busy pizzeria. It contained just the one room so queues would often snake out and round the corner. The crowd was quite a mix of tarted up ladies/ladettes wot lunch, families and business types with huge mobile phones trying to impress and intoxicate clients. I was tempted to take my land phone on a long extension from my home nearby.

Mandala was a legendary hippie store, maybe the only shop to sell organic produce at the time. It sold fair trade goods land had a curious 'medical' section with eastern unguents, herbal potions and unimaginable sanitary products for women. There was a great array of spices, though on asking for hemp seeds I was told they had none, but someone was in the week before asking for some. I queried whether they'd be getting some in, 'no' came the reply, 'there's no demand!'.

Sarah Hall

In 1986 Acorn Road got a new wholefood shop. There was also Milburn's health shop on Mistletoe Road where you could buy 'healthy' crisps on the walk home from West Jesmond School.

System addicts: toys for yuppies

I was in the supermarket one day around 1985 when I saw a man open his briefcase and drag out a device like a house brick, the first mobile phone I'd ever seen. A mobile phone cost around £2000 (the price for a basic phone dropped to £500 in 1988) and the call charges were astronomical. He rang his wife to tell her that peaches were on special offer! I didn't think that mobiles would ever catch on.

The other must-have accessory for the up and coming executive was a Filofax. It was a diary but you could keep other things in there too. Pages for notes, maps, squared paper, zipped pockets, credit card holders and a neat little ruler were all available (at premium prices). You could even buy novels (marketed under the clever name of Filofiction) to clip into your Filofax.

Once you'd crammed all this into the little ring binder it weighed almost as much as a mobile phone. You certainly needed toned biceps to carry both and I suspect this was one of the reasons for the exercise craze that swept Britain in the 1980s.

My boyfriend acquired a Sinclair ZX 81 somewhere around 1983, and spent hours playing with it (sorry, working on it). I think it had 1k of memory, but he scrimped and saved to buy a 4k add-on pack, as well as a better keyboard and a little thermal printer that used silver coloured till rolls. Data was stored on cassette tapes. We had a pretty hi-tech piece of kit, though we still had to attach freezer packs to various components using elastic bands to make sure nothing overheated.

The next computer to grace our home was an Amstrad CPC 464, which had a staggering 64k memory, a proper keyboard, its own colour monitor and an optional floppy disc drive. This was meant for serious stuff. After that my boyfriend, who was by then completely hooked, and teaching IT to adults, went for something custom built.

One night he came home from work carrying something called a modem. He plugged it into the phone and told me not to answer if anyone called at 7pm. Sure enough at 7pm the phone started to ring. There was a click and a whir as it connected to the

North East Times advertises the new up and coming company, Sage Systems, May 1983.

computer. He called me over to see the line of text that was appearing letter-by-letter on the screen. I couldn't understand why anyone would want to type out a message when it would take half the time and effort simply to speak to them on the phone. It was only years later that I realised I'd been watching a very early experiment in e-mail.

Vanessa Histon

They'd have preferred playing Pac-Man, but this was Computers in Education with the Lord Mayor, June 1984.

One Friday evening my friends and I set out for the pub, only to find a great commotion in a corner of the bar. We'd had space invaders for a couple of years, but this was a new game, with a new noise. Welcome to *Pac-Man*! Video games were becoming all the rage, and my mates needed an endless supply of 10p pieces to feed this rival to the pool table with its new range of titles that for once didn't involve zapping aliens, including *Donkey Kong*, as well as *Frogger*, *Centipede*, and the surreal *Burger Time*, where your character was a chef, being chased up and down stairs by food. Fairly soon it became a spectator sport, with every pub having their own 'in house' expert who always seemed to get a high score, presumably due to hours of practice while the rest of us were drinking beer or chatting up girls. Nevertheless, we marvelled at this new found skill, which according to several Hollywood movies at the time, was certain to mean they would be hand-picked to become fighter pilots the instant the impending nuclear war began.

Roland Finch

On their first trip abroad Julie Sloan and her friend took their new Sony Walkmans with them to listen to cassettes on the move.

194

MANIC MONDAY

The Bangles, 1986

Working at Swans

By 1982 less than half of British owned ships were being built in the UK. Shipyards on the Tyne started to close their gates forever – Readheads (1977), Hawthorn Leslie (1982), Palmers Building Dock (1983), The Naval yard at Walker (1985), Neptune (1988) and finally Wallsend in 1993. Despite the 1980s gloom, Swan Hunter built 17 highly complicated ships as well as two aircraft carriers for the Royal Navy, at their five shipyards on the Tyne.

By the early 1980s computers had started to make their mark in the drawing office, changing the nature of draughtsmanship, resulting in increased complexity, 3D plans, and absolute accuracy at a faster rate. Gone were linen plans, measuring scales and a draughtsman's instruments, though thorough shipbuilding knowledge was still required. A young draughtsperson would serve a four-year apprenticeship, backed

Ian Rae

Ark Royal is launched from Wallsend by the Queen Mother, 2 June, 1981.

up by further education up to HND level and beyond. Soon ships were being built by pre-fabricated units and, in time these would become more akin to production line techniques with piping, electrical cable ways etc. fitted prior to being erected on the berth.

The only thing that kept the Tyne yards from closing sooner was the bonanza of replacement ships for the Royal Navy to replace the ones sadly lost in the Falklands War. Royal Naval orders had long been considered a backstop for employment. The Government relented in 1986 to assist shipowners to order in the UK, but it was too little too late. This coincided with the de-nationalisation of the yards, putting them back into private hands once again. However the government's edict that the company should build merchant and warships, meant that as the merchant ship orders dried up more reliance was put on gaining warship orders. Fate contrived to deal a fatal blow with the end to the Cold War, leaving shipbuilders in a dog fight for what orders were on offer.

Ian Rae

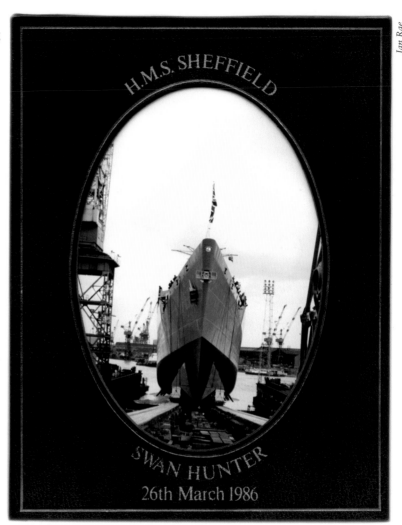

H.M.S. SHEFFIELD

SWAN HUNTER

26th March 1986

The launch of HMS Sheffield, 26 March, 1986. Pride was the main emotion. I'd been working for Swan Hunter for over 25 years and my grandfather started there in 1907, and his son and daughter followed in his footsteps. That was the nature of the industry. The 1980s were the last days of this. I finished in 1993. I worked in the design and engineering dept. (Ian Rae)

I remember hearing on the car radio that there had been an accident on the warship HMS *Ark Royal*, which was being built in the dry docks at Swan Hunter. A freak wind had blown scaffolding down and several workers had fallen into the dry dock. I remember hoping at the time that my dad was all right as he was a plumber in the yards.

Kevin Bell

When I got home he was sitting in his chair white as a ghost. I found out he was the only man involved in the incident and had been blown into to dock from a height of over 30 feet.

He was actually very lucky as the dry dock contained water, which saved his life. However, Dad had never learned to swim and it was only thanks to the labourer that worked with him who managed to grab his collar that he didn't drown. By way of compensation, Dad (*right*) got a new pair of work boots, new overalls and his watch mended!

Kevin Bell

Ice and bikes: cheffing at Gosforth Park

I came to Newcastle in the summer of 1983 to work at the Gosforth Park Hotel under the Austrian manager Kurt Kuen as sous chef to Chef Jeff Bland. It was the era of Newcastle Breweries' ownership. We had a brilliant team of 36 chefs. Nobody would have associated Newcastle with fine dining then. So Gosforth Park was a bit cutting edge. Chef Jeff Bland was one of the best!

The thing that put our chefs on the map was Menu Mystique. It was a five course dinner served on black plates with silver cloches. The customer never saw the menu. You had to discern what you were eating by the taste. It was nouvelle cuisine, but Chef said, 'It's Newcastle, we can't serve tiny portions!' so we made them larger. It was expensive but people came back regularly.

We were involved in lots of promotions including one for Cadbury's Wispa Bar in 1985. We made a 5ft long chocolate cake decorated to look like a Wispa Bar. Then the chef said, 'That's great, they have served it with the ice cream so … make another one tomorrow for the press to photograph! So we ended up making two giant Wispa Bars where one would have been enough.

There was a big panic when Prince Philip came. Three assistant managers were on duty with white gloves and bow ties at 8 o' clock in the morning, all wanting a kipper for Prince Philip. I said 'It only takes one of you, I'll cook it in five minutes'. They were so worried about getting it right they were tripping over each other. I said 'Don't drop it. You will have to wait another five minutes!'

I never got out of the kitchen but I met quite a few of the guests. They came through the kitchen as it was a short cut to the banqueting suite. Bruce Springsteen came through one day. He said 'Come on lads, what do you eat around here?' They said 'Stotty cakes? Pease Pudding? Leek Pudding?' And he said 'Can I have some of that?' He loved it. Kevin Keegan was the same. Towards the end of his time here his family had moved to Southampton so he lived at the hotel during the week. I'd only serve him one meal, and that was Sunday night. The first order on the board on a Sunday night was always for Kevin. It was always steak, baked potato, and salad, which he'd have sent up to his room.

Meatloaf did not meet the restaurant dress code because he wore a frilly shirt open to the waist, with a medallion and hairy chest. They found him an alcove for more privacy.

David Wheatley

In November 1985, after weeks of frantic training, we took part in a charity cycle race on a tandem (we had a transit van too) to bring a bottle of Beaujolais Nouveau from France to the hotel. What a ride back through England! All these big hotels had sponsored us so there'd be a big party every night, with wine. Nobody felt like cycling in the mornings, but it's ok with a hangover if you just keep moving. After the ride over the Tyne Bridge we went up the motorway on the bypass (we weren't supposed to be there) with the van following us and rode straight up the invalid ramp into the foyer of the hotel (*right*). We raised £2000 for Wallsend Boys' Club with that bottle of wine.

The hotel won the contract to produce the buffet luncheon for the opening of the Metro Centre in October 1986. I carved eight blocks of ice; four swans and four eagles. We needed a huge freezer to put them in. At the hotel I had to manhandle the blocks down the lift and into the lorry. It was the same at the Metro Centre. They had promised us a fork lift truck but when we got there, there was no power, or lights for the ice display, so we got car batteries and pond lighting to put behind the sculptures. Sometimes I felt my arms were going to stretch to my ankles. It was about half a mile from the dock into the Centre and back. The trouble with ice under hot lights is … it melts!

I was never bored – in fact I was hardly at home. I didn't get a Christmas, a bank holiday, or a weekend off for years!

By June 1987 I was in New York for a very well paid new job in private service and Chef was working in Scotland.

David Wheatley

David Wheatley

David Wheatley with his rapidly melting ice sculpture, 1986.

TV angsts

In the eighties I worked at Tyne Tees Television and became a parent. I returned to work at the end of March 1983, when my son was 12 weeks old. There was no 'phased return' or part-time hours available to women at that time so it was straight back on the road as a production researcher, working on a series called *Play It Again*.

One of my first research trips on returning to work was to meet and interview Geoff Capes, the 'World's Strongest Man' in Holbeach. I had little idea how far it was to drive but I arranged to conduct the interview at noon then to drive back home the same day. What I hadn't bargained for were the delays owing to the Miners' Strike. This had just started and it put parts of eastern England, particularly around Doncaster, into a kind of lock-down. There were large police teams at roundabouts checking whether any groups of men travelling together, were perhaps on their way to support picket lines or other demonstrations. This gave rise to tail-backs for several miles down the A1. Needless to say I arrived late and was roundly told off for 'failing to turn up' but he reluctantly agreed I could conduct the interview. That was going alright, but the already tense atmosphere worsened when I made the mistake of saying 'I understand you breed budgies'. Furious reposte, 'They are budgerigars, they should never be called budgies!' I almost fell on my knees in apology, fearing we would lose his agreement to do the show and I'd lose my job. Still, he grudgingly showed me the cages where the birds were kept, I gushed my admiration and we were back on track. Then it was back on the road for a faster drive home – there were fewer delays for traffic travelling north, probably because the police only looked for trouble-makers driving south. After all mining was a northern industry.

I also worked on *Nightline*, a live programme with studio audience and phone-in, based on the original *Friday Live* format. One of the programmes was about AIDs, then a new, frightening and misunderstood disease. Many Tyne Tees studio staff, as ignorant and scared by the disease as the public, threatened the transmission because they knew there would be at least one person with AIDs sitting incognito in the studio audience and they feared for their own safety. Negotiations ended after a doctor who treated haemophiliacs explained the risks, which resulted in an agreement that only those willing to do so should work on the studio floor. Thankfully there were enough of them to put the programme on air. While this was happening Tyne Tees' Community Education Department (so many departments in those days!) produced a useful free booklet on the disease. On the night we had some excellent nurses supporting the hectic phone-in – people were so eager for information as well as keen to take part in the conversation. So, what could have been a sensationalist them-and-us debate turned into an interesting, informative and worthwhile programme.

Annie Hodgkiss (Wood)

Rik Walton

Towards the end of the 1970s I was presenting and interviewing for the BBC Radio Newcastle programme *Bedrock*. I had been invited onto the programme by Phil Sutcliffe, one of the programme's founders along with Dick Godfrey, both print journalists. This tied in neatly with my music photography and Phil and I started working together on

Rik (second from right) and the Bedrock team, early 1980s.

commissions for *Sounds* music paper. Most memorable was a couple of days spent with Peter Gabriel, a charming and surprisingly shy man. I remember playing croquet with him, Phil and another photographer on the lawn outside the Holiday Inn. Which other rock star would take a croquet set on tour!

Bedrock ended in the early 1980s. Ian Penman, one of my co-presenters, had gone on to work as a researcher at Tyne Tees Television and somehow got me an audition for the job of presenting Tyne Tees Television's new arts program *The Works*. The competition included one Muriel Gray, fresh from her success on *The Tube*, so my chances were slim! However they did offer me a regular spot reviewing film, television and photography. The programme was recorded, but as we only had very limited studio time for the recording, it was effectively live. It was largely unscripted – the only time I had to use autocue. I was somewhat disconcerted to notice that the woman operating it was knitting at the same time. I did the programme for the first season and managed, largely, to overcome my nerves although I remember our wonderful, and long suffering, producer Heather Ging constantly telling me to smile!

I reviewed an exhibition, organised by Richard Grassick of the Side Gallery, of photographs and newspapers concerning the Miner's Strike, showing the clear manipulation of certain images by the press to discredit the miners and in particular their leader Arthur Scargill. In my review I concurred with the opinions expressed by the gallery and as a result I in turn was accused of bias by ITV who sent an angry letter to Heather Ging. Rather than being angry about this she was delighted!

Rik Walton

Hi-tech at Thomson House

A newspaper office at the beginning of the 1980s didn't look very different from a newspaper office of the 1960s, although a different brand of typewriter might have stood on each reporter's desk. I know this because there's a photo in the *Chronicle and Journal* archive of the poet Basil Bunting when he was working as a sub-editor on *The Journal* business desk in the 1960s. The chair he's sitting on is the same as the one I sat on when I joined the newsroom as a reporter in 1982. A typewriter with a newish ribbon was the coveted journalistic tool. I remember a disgruntled district reporter, visiting head office with an urgent story, hurling typewriter after typewriter into a plastic skip until none remained on the desks.

Writing a story was a laborious process. The first paragraph – the 'intro' – had to be typed on a separate sheet of paper and because you needed a copy, you had to insert carbon paper between two sheets before you started writing. A long story or feature could take several changes of paper and corrections had to be scribbled out. Few bothered with Tipp-Ex. Major events such as the 1982 Falklands War and the Miners' Strike of 1984-5 were covered in this fashion, along with the nitty gritty of day-to-day local reporting. As well as typewriters we had telephones, immobile and without voicemail. Their ring was an old fashioned bell-like clarion call. Along with the constant typewriter clatter, a newsroom was bedlam.

The last deadline on *The Journal* was 2.30am. Reporters phoning in stories had to find a working coin-operated telephone box – no easy feat. I once described an armed siege in Ryton with a small and increasingly disgruntled queue standing outside.

Research was largely dependent on libraries, including the newspaper's own cuttings library where the librarians sat with scissors and glue pots and literally cut-and-pasted the day's stories onto A4 sheets to be filed in brown envelopes (these still exist, an admirable resource for those in the know)

It was in 1985 that I encountered my first fax machine and thought it magic. Suddenly documents could be sent instantly, an improvement on the conventional 'snail mail' which seldom moved fast enough for deadlines.

Then came the big revolution. In 1986 a ferocious dispute began between newspaper magnate Rupert Murdoch and some 6,000 print workers employed at his London national titles. The unionised print workers went on strike and, in a move of swift and ruthless efficiency, Murdoch transferred operations to a brand new site in London's Wapping, which was manned by a new, more compliant workforce. The result of this long and bitter dispute, which Murdoch – backed by the government of Margaret Thatcher – effectively won, was that the newspaper industry would never be the same again. The power wielded to their advantage for years by the print unions suddenly transferred to newspaper managements who swept away the methods of the old and hastened in the digital age.

The company that owned *The Journal and Chronicle* did a deal with a Norwegian company, Norsk Data, so from 1986 we would be writing stories in green text on black screens and, instead of putting bits of type-written paper into the news editor's basket, we would be 'sending' stories digitally. I, for one, felt liberated. No more carbon paper and 'cut-and-paste' became a computer term for rearranging the paragraphs in a newspaper story. Suddenly, it seemed, you could write as fast as you could think and make corrections without scribble.

Arguably there were downsides. Computers couldn't be hurled into skips; neither did they make much noise. On screen you could do more – so were asked to do more. The printers disappeared and with them the possibility of hearty meals in the canteen at midnight for the late reporters.

A quieter, more reverential atmosphere replaced the rackety, rumbustious and – let's be honest – alcohol-fuelled newsroom environment in which reporters had revelled for years. Unions became subdued. Today's young and often non-unionised reporters don't know they're born. Whatever, I wonder, became of Tipp-Ex and Basil Bunting's chair?

David Whetstone

NCJ / Mirrorpix

Reporters using Norsk Data at Newcastle Chronicle and Journal in 1986.

During the 1980s the Newcastle *Evening Chronicle* (and its sister papers *The Journal* and *Sunday Sun*) were in their heyday. Under the editorship of Graeme Stanton, it became one of the most respected evening papers in the country, setting up a thriving school of journalism. I remember the management toilets being hurriedly repainted for a visit by her Royal Highness the Queen Mother, though the reports of the time didn't say whether she used them – or if she ruined her light green coat on the wet paint.

Many great journalists passed through Thomson House on the way to Fleet Street, the BBC, and beyond. And they were always proud to say they had honed their craft with 'the Chron' in Newcastle. Fleet Street is no longer a street of newspapers.

At the start of the decade, the Newcastle papers were produced at speed, a breaking story could be sold on the streets by vendors shouting the headline within an hour. This was an astonishing logistical feat accomplished daily: written by reporters, edited by a team of 'subs' and set in hot metal by an army of printers whose powerful union was the envy of the lesser-paid journalists – and woe betide any impatient sub-editor who tried to speed a story to its deadline by so much as touching the galleys of Linotype or Ludlow headlines, if you did, the whole production process might come to an immediate stop and the deadline would be missed, sales lost and the scoop surrendered to radio or television. By the end of the decade, the printers had been replaced by computers.

Simon Thirsk

Allan Finlay

The Bigg Market, 6.30am, 24 June, 1982. The Journal headlines the Rolling Stones concert at St James Park the day before, and just out of shot, in the Groat Market, the journalists would soon be typing again.

Grott Guitars

Ettrick Scott

Grott Guitars staff outside the shop on Old Eldon Square, mid-1980s.

If it hadn't been for Grott Guitars, and its philanthropist founder, Lionel Gibson, I honestly think I would have starved to death in the late 1980s. Either that, or I'd have been forced to get a proper job, which would have probably been worse. I lost count of the number of times I turned up for work with a skull-crushing hangover and having slept in my clothes, only to find that at least one of my workmates was in a far worse state than me. We weren't natural born shop workers; we were feckless (and largely inept) musicians pretending to interact with the real world, and often failing hilariously.

The fact that Grott took its name from a fictitious chain of shops in the TV show *The Fall and Rise of Reginald Perrin* speaks volumes about the place; in the show, Reggie decides to open a shop that sells rubbish nobody could possibly want – ashtrays with holes in their bottoms, square hula hoops etc – and calls it Grot. Amazingly, Reggie's shops become a runaway success, despite the fact that they sell a load of useless old tat.

Sadly, the same couldn't be said of Lionel's Grott empire; we bought them cheap, piled them high and sold them for a bit more than we'd paid for them. But Grott was never about profit margins or balance sheets, at least, not in the minds of the shop assistants. We had a laugh, honed our risible song-writing skills, insulted each other's hair and dress-sense at length, checked out the talent sunbathing just outside our door if it was a nice day at Old Eldon Square and always, always bought our lunch from off-licences instead of food shops. Anybody who tells you that their schooldays were the best of their life obviously never worked in Grott Guitars …

Sadly, it couldn't last. As the 80s met the 90s, kids were buying decks and DJ equipment more than they bought guitars, and the bottom fell out of the cheapo-cheapo instrument market. I don't think Lionel was too bothered by the crash – he always seemed unflappable and unfazed when it came to unimportant things like running a successful business – and the rest of us were starting to realise that, while you absolutely should spend your twenties playing in a series of crap local bands, it starts to look a bit tragic if you're still doing it in your thirties…

Ettrick Scott

Games, Glue and Gobstoppers – working with kids

My son Gavin was three years old when Lady Diana and Prince Charles were married. Gavin's playgroup at Chapel House and District Community Association were up for celebrating, so all the children were asked to turn up wearing red, white and blue. Bill Steel of Tyne Tees Television was asked to present a commemorative mug to each child.

I was asked by my friend Irene to become a volunteer working with children on the summer holiday play scheme. We'd go to Children's Warehouse, a council-run resource centre that trawled around industrial companies, shops and offices to cadge materials that could be recycled by the children in crafts, model making and costumes. We called ourselves 'Have trolleys will travel,' as we filled shopping trolleys fit to bust with sheets of leather, card, fabric, plastics and much more. Leather was used to make bongo drums, thonging for jewellery and badges. We organised drama sessions, fancy dress and talent contests and kite making. We borrowed bouncy castles that took forever to inflate with a small pump. We had to listen to *Agadoo* by Black Lace over and over again at the discos.

Yvonne Young

This work wasn't without risk; plaster of paris was favourite for causing trouble. We had to saw a child out of a cast he had formed around his hand, we had to use chisels to get it off the lads' toilet ceiling, and it blocked the pipes in the kitchen. Some of the games were cause for concern too. During a game of tug of war, the two teams started to spiral and the rope became wrapped around the neck of a child sitting on the floor. Just as they were about to pull I screamed 'STOP!'

We took the kids to the swimming baths, softplay, Saltwell Park and Washington Wildfowl Park. They enjoyed Otterburn Hall for the adventure activities, archery, canoeing and abseiling.

Yvonne Young

I later became a crèche worker for the Multi-Cultural Arts Group at the old Todd's Nook School. There were no resources, so I made large floor cushions from felt, friends gave me toys that their children had no further use for and I took along puppets, stories and rhymes. The group was very popular with mothers and I could be caring for up to ten under 5s on my own (this was before the 1989 Children's Act). Before long another worker joined me, Firdos Khan, who is still my friend today.

The day I started work, in April 1986, the Americans had bombed Colonel Gadaffi's Libya. As many of the women who attended the groups were from that area, I wondered if I would have any customers, but we had a full house. The women came from Africa, China, Iraq, Iran, Pakistan and India. I experienced difficulties with languages at the beginning. I remember a child asking me 'Pani … pani?' She was asking for water. So I realised that I would have to create a resource to deal with this. I made a set of cards for each language, drew a picture on each and wrote the name of the object. Parents helped by adding the relevant word in their own language. I used these with the children and often they would laugh at my pronunciation of a word, then they would correct me: a true learning process for us both.

There were many crossed-wire incidents. On one occasion an Indian woman and an English woman were looking at a photo of a goat. 'Billy goat' said the English woman 'No, Billy – cat' said the Indian lady. This went back and forth for a while until someone pointed out that 'billi' is the word for cat in Hindi. I also stumbled upon the meaning of words such as 'hathi', which means elephant, when I made a card for this animal. So, the leader of the troupe of elephants in Jungle Book is simply Colonel Elephant!

As crèche worker, I followed the group around schools in the west end such as Westgate Hill, Canning Street, Wingrove and Moorside. There were trips to Wallington Hall, Knaresborough, art galleries and museums. Dancers often visited the group, as well as women from different cultures who came to teach new skills.

Yvonne Young

While I was at school I got my first job working for Paul's the clothes shop because a friend's sister already worked in the office there. It was a warehouse and was in Rye Hill near where the casino is now. We were employed to put tickets on clothing for Clock House at C&A. I was 13 or 14 so I had to get school to sign a permit to say I could work. We had to unpack boxes of garments, put the tickets on and pack them up again. There were six of us and we worked all day Saturday and all day Sunday and got £15 for the two days' work.

Sharon Reeve

Saturday was the only day I wanted to leave my two young children to go to work as my husband took over the child care. The three of them would drop me off at Littlewoods for 8.30. He would park the car in town then all three, husband, son and daughter would appear at Littlewoods for their cooked breakfast; they had already had cereal at home, but this felt like a treat. They would be back at 5.15 to collect me. The shop opened at 9am and it was always busy. I worked on the deli counter and always knew when the DFDS ferries were in as the store was full of Scandinavians. They always bought in bulk, struggling under the weight of full trays of bacon. This seemed strange to me, but they said it was much cheaper than back in their own countries. The deli counter was always busy but especially from 4.45 until 5pm, when the store was due to close. Our regulars know that most deli items would be reduced at the end of the day, so they would hover to see if their favourite savoury pie, flan, cut meats or cheese were going to be a bargain. They'd ask for one slice or a few grams of cheese, then, when you'd cut it or weighed it. they would change their minds and walk away. I always have sympathy with shop assistants as 'the customer is always right' or certainly was then, and boy did they try your patience.

Pat Rogerson

On the dole

After being made redundant from Hepworth's the tailors in 1980 I started working as a 'Blowpipe' operator, which is a semi-skilled glassblower, at the Thermal Syndicate in Wallsend. As work dried up we moved around the factory doing various other jobs, not always knowing what or even who, the final product was for. My last move in the factory was to the Chirton works on Norham Road. Here we checked small quotes rods, which we passed through feeler gauges. If they stuck we rejected them. I think we tested about 450 an hour. We were told these rods were for Rolls Royce for use in the rotor blades of the engines for Tri-Star plant.

One morning we heard on the radio that Tri-Star had been cancelled. An hour later the foreman came round to say overtime was off, by dinner time we where told we would be going on a shorter working week then by 4 o'clock we had a union meeting to discuss redundancies and the closure of the Chirton factory. Needless to say before the end of the month we were all out of work.

Kevin Bell

I spent almost exactly half of the 1980s unemployed and signing on at Swan House. The summer of 1980 saw all four men in my family out of work, leaving only my mother not having to sign on, as we all did, at the same box, on the same day, at the same time. The prospect of a family outing for the purpose of signing on the dole was not an attractive one, so we would usually split into three parties, dad leaving first, Steve shortly afterwards and Chris and me together, fashionably late.

Simon Donald

Working for Berger Paints

After six months out of work on £7.70 a week dole, in March 1980 I started work at the Resinous Chemical plant in Dunston (next to where the Metro Centre was about to be built) but a walk, a train, another walk, then an unreliable bus before an even longer walk to get there prompted me to look for a job somewhere else. Fortunately I got a job in the Elastomers division at the Berger Paints factory in Shieldfield, Newcastle.

I started in March 1981. I remember my first day going to work, crossing the bridge at Byker on the Metro and seeing that white, square-faced clock on the five-storey building. (It's still there, but now it wears a pointy hat!) It was quite a large site that manufactured industrial and marine paint. The five-storey block had laboratories on most floors and also housed paint manufacturing. The office block was across the road with more paint manufacture behind and the elastomers manufacturing next to that. My CV would eventually say 'we developed and manufactured synthetic rubber compounds to seal aircraft fuel tanks, seal insulated glazing units and encapsulate electrical mains cables and gas pipes'. Many of the products we made were approved to Civil Aviation and MoD specifications and it was quite amazing that a Concorde was sitting on the ground waiting for me to sign the approval certificate.

Allan Finlay

Concorde, Newcastle Airport, 2 September, 1985. With an accident at Manchester Airport in 1985, British Airways grounded some of its aircraft and so they had to use Concorde on the Newcastle to Heathrow route for a short while. I managed to get a return ticket, so I can say I have flown on Concorde, though sadly not Supersonic!

(The first Concorde flights from Newcastle were chartered by Newcastle Chronicle and Journal in 1982. In 1983 special flights were advertised for 28 and 29 August at £195 one way to London or £230 return. Or you could book a supersonic trip over the North Sea for £325.)

Barrow boys

We are the oldest street trading family in Newcastle. Before the 1980s my barrow was at the corner of Nelson Street – there would be about 20 barrows there. Then I went to Brunswick Place, but without a licence we'd be chased all over the place by the police! It all changed in 1981 when the council actually gave us a licence to trade, which was a magnificent thing to have. We were delighted. It made such a difference because before the licence we had to trade illegally – my mother even had to go to prison – and my grandmother and I kept fighting for legalisation. Since 1981 my barrow has stood on Northumberland Street. Today I am chairman of the Barrow Traders Association.

Albert Sayers

A street trader on Brunswick Place, summer 1983. Woolworth's would survive until 1985.

Holiday job

I worked at Thomson's travel bureau in 1981. There were not many jobs about so I was very pleased to get that one as I was interested in travel. I was the junior in the office, so unfortunately I didn't get a cheap holiday, but I thought it was very exciting planning a trip to Jamaica for my boss, sending telexes and letters.

It was a big thing for us to even think of going abroad on a holiday. My friend worked at Callers Pegasus so eventually we were able to have our first holiday

Julie Sloan

Above, top office technology at Thomson's, 1981.
Left, about to board at Newcastle Airport.

Camera work

I photographed over 50 productions at Newcastle Playhouse during the 1980s. It was demanding work. I tried to read the script in advance, and would often attend late rehearsals as well as the technical rehearsal in order to pinpoint moments in the show that would make good images. I knew the director was not going to stop the dress rehearsal for me! The real work began at the dress, usually on Wednesday night. I would take between two and 300 photographs. Sometimes the rehearsal would carry on into the wee hours, but nevertheless I had to go home, develop the films and prepare contact sheets for the following morning. The director would choose 12 images, which I would enlarge to 20x16ins, mount and hang on the wall of the theatre for opening night on Thursday. No opportunity to retake the photos so it could be nerve wracking!

I saw many fine shows at the Playhouse during the 80s, until the company's ill-judged move to the New Tyne Theatre. Highlights for me were the trilogy of Arthur Miller plays directed by John Blackmore. *Death of a Salesman* was particularly powerful, indeed, I had to stop taking photos ten minutes before the end of the rehearsal as my eyes misted up and I couldn't see to focus!

There were some strong musicals staged, including *Cabaret* and *Chicago*, as well as adaptations of Catherine Cookson novels, and the premiere of Pam Gems' *Pasionaria*, the story of Isidora Dolores Ibárruri Gómez. During the rehearsal period for this play, regular rewrites arrived in the post from Gems, who was at her holiday home in Spain – no email in those days! It drove the director round the twist. Ken Hill premiered his version of the *Phantom of the Opera* in 1984. This was the inspiration for Andrew Lloyd Webber's adaptation.

Musicians played regularly in the downstairs bar, and in 1988 the theatre hosted the revived Newcastle Jazz Festival, which I was asked to photograph. George Melly was due to play the opening concert. The festival

Rik Walton

Phantom of the Opera, Playhouse, 1984.

organisers had arranged for an open topped bus with a jazz band to meet him at the station, the idea being to drive through the streets publicising the festival. They must have been a bit short staffed as they asked me if I would meet George off the train and put him on the bus. George had clearly been enjoying liquid refreshment on the journey and was in ebullient form. I told him a bus was waiting for him outside. However, he had decided he could get a better deal on his return ticket, which meant we had to queue for forty minutes to make the changes and save him £10! Meanwhile the bus and the band waited patiently outside.

The Playhouse became a second home to me in the 80s. There was a resident company and the atmosphere was friendly, there was always someone I knew in the bar. During this period many young actors who went on to fame and fortune had their first professional opportunities, among them Julia Sawalha, John Hannah, Josie Lawrence, Kevin Whately, Ron Culbertson, and Miranda Richardson, who starred in the European premiere of David Mamet's play *Edmund*.

Rik Walton

Rik Walton

The late great George Melly, and the Metro Radio bus, 1988.

I worked as a photographer's assistant at Tony Gilbert's studio in Low Friar Street. We took photographs for Procter and Gamble, Fly Mo, the Co-op, for TV ads, and for Northern Rock. I went along in 1985 with my portfolio and the photographer, Frank Unwin, liked one of my shots. For a year after that it was my job to load film backs, load cameras, set up lights, get props and generally make clients, models and the photographer (who was trying to give up smoking) at ease. Frank was enthusiastic and good with people, a David Bailey for the North East. In fact he had worked in London before Newcastle. The studio was a good experience, a place to take my own photographs on days off. At Christmas time we would take food shots for newspaper ads, eating the food if it survived. The artistic director from the ad agency that commissioned the photography studio would spend a while getting the photographer or stylist (or me) to arrange the shot until it became almost surreal, there were only a finite number of places a streamer could go.

I met Martin Stephenson of the Daintees on the 194 bus going from Washington to Newcastle. He was a striking figure with his hat. I photographed them at the Riverside, at Northumbria University and at the Jumping Hot Club, a roots music venue downstairs in the Bridge Hotel.

I also did some work with Children's Warehouse on Pilgrim Street. They sourced free materials such as paint, card, tubes and fabric, from various factories that would just throw the stuff away, and recycled it for a small fee to playgroups and youth clubs who would use the materials to make sculptures. My contribution to these recyclers was to run a photography workshop for junior age children and provide an image that would get publicity for them. The image I took for a poster showed a couple of teenagers hanging around a Metro station sharing a cigarette, perhaps showing the futility of life for them, and promoting community youth activities.

Juan Fitzgerald

Juan Fitzgerald

Juan captures the atmosphere at the Riverside.

215

I was working as a waitress in a cocktail bar …

I was a student at Newcastle Polytechnic and needed a part-time job so I thought I would try my hand at bar work. I went to the job centre and found several bars were looking for staff. Hanrahan's on the Quayside paid the best (£2.95 per hour). The manager asked me if I had any bar experience and when I replied that I hadn't … he said I could start the following week! So, on 29 March 1989, I started working behind the bar and learned how to make cocktails. On Friday and Saturday nights, the bar was extremely busy (one night Jimmy Nail was there). I couldn't believe how people would queue for ages to get into a crowded place then spend lots of money on drinks, but for the bar staff it was great as we often made lots of tips. The cocktails were delicious but very potent. We had cocktail training sessions 3-7pm on Sundays when the bar was shut. This was a chance to make every cocktail on the menu and try them. Needless to say I would be very tipsy afterwards! One of my favourites was the famous Mars Bar

Angela Merritt

Angela (second from left), and friends sample some potent cocktails.

cocktail made in a blender with Kahlua, cream and coconut cream served in a high ball glass and garnished with a fun sized Mars Bar. Sometimes we went nightclubbing after the bar closed. In fact, life was like one long party.

Angela Merritt (née Wong)

Hanrahans, 1988. The mishmash of styles from Tiffany-style stained glass to exposed brickwork and Victorian-style dark wood, was typical of late 1980s bars. If you ordered one of the many cocktails priced at £2.50 you might choose a Hang 10 which was vodka, Malibu, blue curaçao, lemon juice, pineapple juice and cream; or a Chilli-Hill-Billy which was green crème de menthe, Southern Comfort, Advocaat, cream and lemonade.

Policing the PM

In 1980 I became a village bobby in Northumberland and Newcastle became a place I went to work overtime during major events, when additional police officers were drafted in. I spent one miserably overcast day, with many other police officers, earning time and a third at the Civic Centre when the Prime Minister, Margaret Thatcher paid a visit. We had been warned on pain of death to be especially smartly turned out as you never know where an appreciative Prime Minister might go walkabout, in the gaze of the world's media, to express her gratitude. My allocated spot was outside on Sandyford Road. The grey mass of concrete and square glass windows that make up the Civic Centre quickly lost its appeal as I stared at it. It was the opposite of standing outside St James Park – lonely. There was no crowd to nod to as they passed. So, as instructed, I stood, waiting for something suspicious or exciting to happen. It never did.

The threat of Irish terrorism weighed heavily on those in charge of security. After several hours of standing, a stressed looking senior officer appeared and after some complaints allowed a group of us who had not moved for hours to go into the Civic Centre for a hot drink. As we queued inside the warmth of the building for our refreshment, the same senior officer came in and complained of people skiving and sent us all back out where we stood for several more hours looking at the civic centre again. As I walked back to my position I remarked to a colleague that I hoped they had at least given

Margaret Thatcher at the Civic Centre, 23 March 1985, shortly after the end of the Miners' Strike.

Mrs Thatcher a cup of tea during her visit as her day would have been nearly as long as ours.

The end of the visit was marked by a flash of blue light and a motorcade zoomed away from the Civic Centre. It occurred to me that she had not had the chance to look around my beautiful city. I think she would have liked it. Nor had she had the opportunity to admire my freshly pressed uniform. I thought I saw the wave of a hand as the motorcade left but I was too far away to see who it belonged to. In any event that was as close as I ever got to meeting Margaret Thatcher. By that time I would have settled for the tea.

Graham Pears

The Specials

It all began when I saw an advertisement for the Northumbria Police Special Constabulary in *Neighbourhood News*. Several months after I had applied I received my collar number and began the training programme. The Induction Course at Ponteland HQ was very hard work so the day of the passing out parade was a very proud one for me.

Then the fun really started, if that's what you can call it! My first tour of duty was on a nice bright evening and I was on foot patrol with a regular constable who was great – helpful and kind. However, he had a good laugh when suddenly the radio barked into life. The message was 'LB calling 5574', which I totally ignored! After a couple more calls, I realised that my colleague was laughing because that was my number, and it was me who was being called – how I wished the ground would open up and swallow me!

A really important milestone was my first arrest. A young lad was being really silly on Shields Road. I had recently been transferred to the Byker sub-division. I arrested him and took him off to Clifford Street, dreading having to go before the Custody Sergeant to explain why I had made the arrest. Much to my relief, the lad admitted he had been drunk and disorderly and my heart stopped racing. He was fined £25 and costs – a very expensive night out for him!

Some weeks later a colleague and I were checking the backs of premises on Shields Road, when we heard thumping. Two lads were trying to kick in the rear door of an insurance office. We challenged them and they both jumped onto the roof of the premises and tried to hide behind the chimney stack! One of them began to jump from garage roof to garage roof, and I followed his progress. He eventually tried to hide, but sadly for him, I could still see his backside sticking out from behind the wall. He was arrested on suspicion of attempted burglary. His friend, however, decided to put on a show for another five minutes before he realised that he was going nowhere. So they were both taken off to the 'nick'.

The next big arrest happened when I was on duty with my Specials colleague David. We were stopped by a taxi driver who reported that a group of six men had smashed Greggs shop window and had stolen the display of goodies that had been prepared for the next morning. We commandeered the taxi to take us to the scene. Passers-by told us that the people responsible were only a hundred yards down the road. We caught up with them and told them that we wanted a word with them! Well, we were absolutely amazed when, as one, they all turned to the wall, put their hands up against it and spread their legs. They must have been watching too many American cop shows on television! Various delicacies were soon produced from coat pockets. We had struck gold, with six arrests on suspicion of burglary!

Tom Smith, Special Constable

I had wanted to be a police officer for as long as I could remember, having had a lifelong interest in true crime. Unfortunately, being only just over five feet six and a half inches tall, this was not a possibility. Even in the 1980s, the height restriction of five feet eight inches was enforced rigidly. I got a job as a Court Clerk working for Northumbria Police. During the interview the Special Constabulary was mentioned so I decided to apply, and was accepted.

My first duty in uniform was on a busy Saturday afternoon on foot patrol on Shields Road with an experienced Special Constable. I vividly recall my sense of pride, terror and trepidation. What happened? Absolutely nothing!

One particular incident sticks in my mind. I was on match duty with a Regular colleague. At 2.15pm we were walking through Eldon Square Shopping Centre when we heard shouting and encountered three men. One of the men, a well-known shoplifter began shouting threats and trying to goad my colleague into a fight. Passers-by were clearly shocked, so we arrested him. The lad pushed the officer in the chest, my first ever experience of someone assaulting a colleague, but we eventually got the youth out of the shopping centre into Blackett Street. He then began to struggle violently and in spite of being subdued by my colleague he continued lashing out with fists and feet.

I became a Special in 1989 after realising that if I wanted to do something to combat things like phone box vandalism, I'd better join up. I was 49, but was accepted for training and began a thoroughly useful and enjoyable ten years. (Douglas Bond)

My colleague was knocked to the ground. At that time, Specials were not issued with truncheons, and the two of us only had one personal radio between us, which my colleague was carrying, so I was unable to summon aid. I was left to try to restrain the man on my own. The situation was becoming desperate, so eventually I called out for help. Surprisingly, I managed to get the man to the ground and to my everlasting gratitude, a man in the crowd came forward and promptly sat on the offender! This gave me the opportunity to slip the handcuffs on. In court our good Samaritan received a well-deserved commendation from the magistrate.

David Hinshaw

Bookwork

I had six months' maternity leave when I had my daughter in 1980. I came back to work at Fenham library and then moved to Denton Burn. It took about an hour and a quarter to get there from Four Lane Ends but I loved Denton Burn; it was friendly and busy and in the centre of the shops. Lots of people came to borrow books. Scotswood, where I also worked was awful. We shut the library at lunchtime and I had to stay in the staffroom by myself. It was haunted! Books would fall off the shelves by themselves.

There was no automation; we used the old Brown system of cards. I was envious of people who had lovely long nails and could go through it very quickly. I could never do that. At night you had to do all the aligning and arranging of

Kath Cassidy

Kath, left, and colleagues at Fenham Library, early 1980s. The spread wasn't for the customers!

the tickets and counting, and putting them into fiction, non fiction, junior, junior non fiction … so everything that had been taken out during the day was put into sequence. I used to dread it when people couldn't find a book or lost a ticket as finding them was so laborious; you had to start going through all the trays. Everything was done by hand. You just sat and wrote everything. It was nice though as there were lots of staff and you'd talk to people while you were looking for the tickets and the books, lots of time to chat. Library work was well paid in comparison to similar jobs because there was extra money for night and Saturday working. And I got about five weeks holiday a year, and an annual increment.

Kath Cassidy

My first pay packet was £220.22 for the month. It was 1983, I was 17 and I worked at Jesmond Library. We wore gingham overalls and Dr Scholl sandals. The older librarians were called 'Miss' and they favoured twin sets and pearls with half glasses. We were still using the old manual Brown system and changing over to the computerised system involved a lot of writing! Before the system went live we had to copy all the borrowers' membership details from little cards onto forms. We had to issue all the books on the old system onto the computer when it went live. It was a massive job.

There were cassettes at Jesmond when I started. CDs arrived in the late 80s and they used to get stolen.

Barbara Bravey

Librarian Alan Wallace proudly displays the audio cassettes available to borrow from the City Library. They proved very popular. In May 1984 300 video cassettes were added to lending stock. They cost £1 a day to borrow and the most popular titles were Michael Jackson's Thriller, Raiders of the Lost Ark, and Superman III.

In the summer of 1989 Newcastle library workers who were NALGO members came out on strike along with local government workers all over the country. Janice Hall, second left, brought her two children, and described it as everyone coming together in a common cause. Picketing involved many members. Pay had fallen way behind average national earnings. NALGO achieved a 12% rise through the campaign.

Newcastle City Libraries Book Buzz in 1984. It was a huge success, visiting primary schools across the city, particularly those not near a branch library. In the summer holidays it was taken to different parts of the city for story sessions, face painting, and other activities. It was always under threat from spending cuts.

MAKING YOUR MIND UP

Bucks Fizz, 1981

The student life

1986 – decision time – Aston University or Newcastle Polytechnic? Brummies or Geordies? Concrete Bull Ring or iconic Tyne Bridge? Jasper Carrott or Jimmy Nail? I came to my open day in Newcastle unsure what to expect, but quickly realised that I had stumbled across a vibrant, friendly and exciting place – albeit a bit rough around the edges. I shunned the traditional landmarks (Eldon Square, Monument, Bigg Market), preferring the more alternative scene. Yellow bagged vinyl from Volume Records, breaking bands and Big Niall's tunes at the Riverside, pints of Scotch at the Broken Doll, Barley Mow and Egypt Cottage, student dives in The West End – who could want more? I loved it and am still here 27 years later – almost an adopted Geordie!

Craig Merritt

Craig Merritt

By 1989 three years of being a student in Newcastle had taken its toll of Craig, third from the left, at the Egypt Cottage with friends. He was unable to leave.

224

On my first day as a student I arrived at what was then a converted convent in Sandyford and, after waving off my parents, I decided to walk into Newcastle to see if I could find a familiar face from my old school back in Derbyshire. Needless to say that was a bit like looking for a needle in a haystack. These first few days of feeling a bit homesick soon turned into the best days of my life.

Weekday nights became hectic and in my youth I managed to cope well with late nights and 9 o'clock lectures. Weekends were rather more sedate. It was almost an unwritten rule that students didn't venture into the city at weekends; we were preoccupied with the 'Poly bop' or wandering around Fenham looking for someone's house party. One of my favourite haunts was the Jewish Mother, where a £3 ticket got you entry and a plate of food as well as some great bands on stage – like Under the Doctor. There were many nights pooling energy into drinking bottles of 1080 or some other cider to get a free t-Shirt! I remember a great impromptu Friday lunch at a bar next to the City Hall sharing beers and deciding it was far too much fun there than to return to a Law seminar!

Sarah Harrison (née Bond)

Newcastle was incredibly friendly. Everyone you met outside the University, as soon as they heard your accent asked, 'Where are you from? Do you like it here?' I have memories of the Bigg Market in the winter, of the local girls, in short, short white mini skirts and white boots with tassels, no tights. The blokes were all in shirts with their sleeves rolled up, while we had jumpers and coats and scarves on. On the last bus home to Fenham on a Friday or Saturday night – there was ALWAYS someone dressed up as a bumble bee.

In the first year I lived on the fifth floor of Eustace Percy Hall, with a view of the blue star on the Scottish & Newcastle brewery

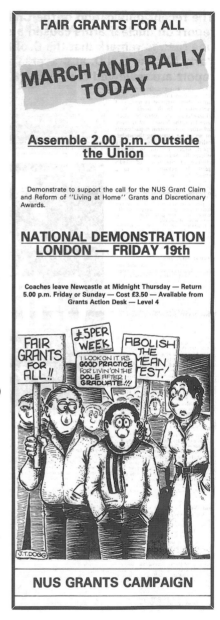

The Courier, 17 November, 1982

(and appropriate smells at brewing time). The food was dire. Someone walked out of a third floor window when we lived there. But apparently he was so drunk he didn't try to break his fall. They said that was why he survived. He just flopped on the ground.

I remember the porters, especially a little fat man, I think he was called Bob. They were funny, grumpy, kind and helpful and didn't miss a trick. They must have seen everything in their time – door locks blocked with spaghetti, a cow in the lifts, sick all over the back stairs, doors swapped so the room numbers didn't go in order. I once got into a lift with a friend, and his room door was also in the lift going up and down! Once a group of boys swapped two boys' rooms while they were out. Every detail was perfect, every book in place. It was unbelievable. They didn't bother to swap back and lived in each other's rooms until the end of the year.

Kevin Keegan's testimonial match happened at St James Park when we lived at Castle Leazes in 1984. We didn't get in, but it was amazing. The crowd roared right through the match and at the end the ground actually shook.

In my second year, we lived in an awful house in Fenham. There were slug trails across the downstairs carpets and when we put salt down to stop them, it crystallised, soaking up the damp from the wet floors and carpets. At one point the toilet wastepipe broke and we had sewage coming down the inside of the kitchen wall. We had to use the toilets at Newcastle Bowl last thing at night and first thing in the morning. We had all sorts of problems with the landlord.

The Celtic Society was set up in around 1986 and bent the Union Society's rules to breaking point. Everyone who attended a ceilidh was given free membership which ran into the hundreds, giving the Celtic Society entitlement to considerable extra funding! For a while, the Celtic Society and India Forum ran joint events that filled the event halls to capacity. The

Newcastle University and Union, 1980.

society leaders have gone on to great entrepreneurial heights and the Union changed the funding rules!

The late Piers Merchant was the local MP. He said he could live on the equivalent of unemployment benefit, failed miserably and lost his seat at the next election in 1987, not least because of the student voters. We went out as a house to the polling station together.

We were the generation who grew up knowing no Prime Minister except Margaret Thatcher. She became Prime Minister when we were 14 and was still there when we graduated. It was like some kind of lid on the world that you either accepted as inevitable or had to fight. I remember sit-ins happening when we were students and a friend coming home saying she'd been dragged out of a building by police. You had very little faith in organisations like the police unless you were ultra-conservative. It was probably asking for a shout-down to say you were a Tory supporter. A lot of students had very little tolerance for Conservative politics. I knew one boy who was openly Tory. We thought he was a nutter.

The paternoster lifts in Claremont Tower – who can forget them? The older students used to go up and come back down doing a handstand, just to freak the Freshers!

Julia Norman

WOMEN'S ROOM

Level 6

Coffee ☆ tea
conversation
books ☆ magazines
contacts ☆ workshops
self-defence

Next Women's Group Meeting
TONIGHT
Thursday, 13th October
7.00 p.m.
ALL WOMEN WELCOME

"OH! THAT EXPLAINS THE DIFFERENCE IN OUR PAY"

Clare Guthrie, Women's Officer

Diverse opportunities for student activities existed in Newcastle University Union. Courier, 1988.

I set off for Newcastle Poly in September 1989. Housing benefit was available during the first year but was axed after that (the last of the student 'extras' to go, long after supplementary benefit, train tickets and the pots, pans and bedding allowance!).

We benefited from full-time contact hours and tutors who were always available. The library had qualified staff on every floor and there were plenty of seats, so it didn't need to be open 24 hours a day.

B.A. Brown

My PhD research topic was the study of atmospheric pollution on the rural-urban fringe of Tyneside.

Every week I took the department's minibus out to collect my rainwater and particulate samples and more than once I locked myself out of the minibus and had to find a phone box to ask a technician to come and bail me out. Health and safety wasn't an issue 30 years ago. At one site I had to climb ladders to get to the roof where my sampling equipment was sited and I would often work very late on my own in the lab using dangerous chemicals, sometimes staying all night. Occasionally a night porter would call in, but only to see why the lights were on.

I spent hours at the Newcastle Weather Centre hand copying data from charts. Taking notes from journals was just as laborious before computers. Data analysis was a marathon: precious slots had to be booked so I could punch data onto cards, which were then read on a card reader. Later I could collect the results from Claremont Tower in the form of reams of 'njfm3' data output, which had to be carefully checked. If I made a single error when punching the cards I had to do it all again! Creating graphs and maps was a painstaking process using Letraset and Rötring pens on my homemade light table.

The date for my viva was set was rather close to the expected arrival date of my first child. Four days after the viva my daughter arrived – she joined me three months later on my PhD graduation photographs.

Jennifer Brake (née Warren, formerly Mageean)

I was Bursar for the Castle Leazes Halls of Residence at Newcastle University from 1982 – the days when students organised their own entertainment, Junior Common Rooms and Senior Common Rooms held regular events, and staff and students actually had fun.

A typical academic year in the life of Castle Leazes went something like this …

The day the freshers arrived at Castle Leazes usually created traffic chaos in Spital Tongues and Barrack Road. The congestion was compounded if Newcastle United were playing a home game. There were queues of cars, filled with anxious parents, proud grandparents and nervous freshers, all keen to inspect the new accommodation. On many occasions the family dog came too. With over 1,116 residents, the halls were soon buzzing.

Hall Balls were always terrific events and members of hall staff were frequently invited by the students as guests. At one Hall Ball it was decided by the JCR committee that they would chuck the senior warden (a physics professor) into a cold bath – fully clothed in his evening suit. He was to be swiftly followed by the Accommodation Services Manager, who when hearing what was in store for him, legged it out of a fire exit door and climbed a 6ft fence.

Hall Balls in those days were spectacular events with student committees working hard to transform the fairly austere premises into pleasure palaces. Local firms would be approached by the students to donate or lend things for the event. I drove down to the Swan Hunter yards with a couple of students to collect several metres of naval flags and heavy duty ropes for a nautical themed ball.

The dress sense of the female agriculture students at these events was inspirational – ball gowns and Doc Martens with fishnet tights and occasionally a pitchfork. But the most memorable outfit was worn by the son a

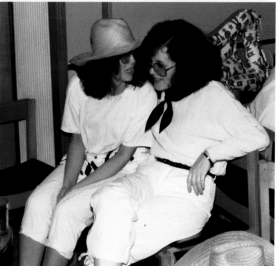

Party time at the Hall Ball, mid-1980s.

Hélène Dolder

prominent Archbishop, who went to the 'Vicars and Tarts' event dressed as a testicle – obviously to have a 'ball!' Local bands were a big feature at these events, especially the East Side Torpedoes who were really popular with the students.

When it snowed the enterprising students would head for nearby Cow Hill, armed with dinner trays they had smuggled out of the dining rooms, for sledging competitions. It took the catering manager some time to work out why his stocks of trays rapidly diminished in the winter months.

Hélène Dolder

It was anything but a rosy-fingered dawn. There was a distinct chill in the air at the start of a snowy Rag Day in 1982. Students from the Classics Department huddled under the Arches, waiting for Dr Peter Jones to launch the departmental 'Homer-athon'. Dr Jones had decided to swell the Rag Day coffers by organising a sponsored recitation of Homer's Odyssey in Classical Greek. The bard took his position at the bema, or reading desk, and began to declaim the tale of Odysseus and his return from Troy. At the end of his oration, Dr Jones prepared to pass the baton to members of his Classical flock. Faces turned as white as the snow on the rooftops – was this a case of pre-performance nerves or merely a sudden attack of acute frostbite? Many of us still remember our epic moment. The Homer-athon was good fun and raised funds for a worthy cause.

David and Caroline Gill

David and Caroline Gill

Having a drink with Julie Christie

The early 1980s was a time of east-west tension. Margaret Thatcher and Ronald Reagan were stoking up fears of an imminent attack by the Eastern Bloc. The Conservative Government issued a leaflet titled *Protect and Survive* to all households in 1980 as part of a programme of improvements to Civil Defence. In response, a whole generation of Tyneside youth flocked to join CND and united around the slogan Protest and Survive. NATO military policy at the time was to use tactical nuclear weapons on Day 5 of any such insurgency. The University TND (Tyneside for Nuclear Disarmament) Soc started in October 1980. Several of us in the science department got together to provide music at demos and events.

One of our first public performances, in September 1980, was to a crowd of hundreds in Eldon Square at a rally addressed by actress Julie Christie. Later, Julie bought us a round of Guinness at the Three Bulls Heads, which I have never forgotten!

STOP THE WAR GAMES

Rally against the massive NATO exercises in Europe during September.

Saturday 13th September
12 noon
Old Eldon Square
Newcastle upon Tyne

Speakers from: Churches, Trade Union M... Peace Movement, Anti-Nu... and others.

A film show at Ty... will follow in the...

In 1983 Julie Christie (right) was back in Newcastle at the Tyneside Film Festival. She was interviewed for the Newcastle University student newspaper, Courier, by Arts Editor Steve Waring, and photographer Ian Jackson. She said 'The face of Britain is changing into something very nasty and it's up to us all to look at it and say ... Do I want this to happen to my country?'

David Anstead

Dave Anstead, 1981.

Ian Jackson for Courier

We formed the Backfire Bombers, an acoustic band specialising in anti-nuclear protest songs. We were prominent at CND events in the North East and London. After more changes of line-up, our new band, Day 5 (the name from NATO policy) was formed in the summer of 1981.

There were rallies and events to protest against what were perceived as inadequate measures and a frightening build up of nuclear arms. In May 1981 TND and Tyneside Trade Councils held a May Day rally in Nixon Hall, Ellison Place, with MP Eric Heffer, and it was followed by several days of events.

David Anstead

Day 5 performing at The Lonsdale, Jesmond in 1981. Left Dave Anstead on bass and right John Toscano, vocals. Other band members were Kon Piergies, drums, and Dave Raeside, guitar.

Adverts in Courier catered for a student's every need.

YOU WIN AGAIN

The Bee Gees, 1987

The beautiful game

The 1980s was far from being one of the greatest periods in Newcastle United's colourful 131 year history. Yet, as is the Magpies' way, there were plenty of headlines on and off the field as the 1980s unfolded. The period started in mediocrity then ended losing a play-off to Sunderland, of all clubs, and with the famous Black'n'Whites in a fragile position, rapidly deteriorated. In between those low points supporters did witness moments of pleasure as a unique bond was created with ex-England skipper Kevin Keegan and were able to appreciate the genius of a trio of home-grown superstars in the making; Chris Waddle, Peter Beardsley and Paul Gascoigne. It was a roller-coaster of emotion, although more frustration than delight.

During seasons 1980-81 and 1981-82, the Black'n'Whites struggled to build a team good enough to make a sustained bid for promotion back to the top flight. However, during the summer of 1982 the Geordies, as a second-tier club, pulled off a

Special K takes on Chelsea, 1982.

233

sensational coup by bringing the biggest name of the English game, Kevin Keegan, to Tyneside. As a result during 1982-83 and 1983-84 the spotlight was back on Newcastle United as Keegan led the way. And Special K ended his career on a high, guiding United to promotion in an entertaining fashion ... the first part of a remarkable union between player and fans.

Back with the élite in the First Division, despite managerial upheaval that saw Arthur Cox, Jack Charlton and Willie McFaul take charge, United consolidated their position and for a while looked to be building a decent side, but financial constraints off the pitch and a resultant lack of perceived ambition saw their biggest assets head south over the Tyne Bridge one by one – Waddle to Tottenham, Beardsley to Liverpool and then Gazza moved to White Hart Lane too. The club tried to appease supporters by bringing in Mirandinha, the first Brazilian to show his talent in top English football, but a transfer spree failed to halt a slide. With another new man in charge, Jim Smith, the club tumbled into the relegation mire and were relegated during 1988-89.

By season 1989-90 United were on the decline, losing a promotion play-off to their Wearside rivals. The proud but now ailing Newcastle United were almost bankrupt and in turmoil both in the dressing-room and Boardroom. The Magpie Group were waiting in the wings, ready to push for a complete and long overdue takeover. And that set United's quite remarkable story into another pulsating chapter.

Paul Joannou, Official Historian to Newcastle United

Peter Beardsley

The 80s was an amazing time for me. Kevin Keegan is like a god in this city so to come back to Newcastle in 1983 and play alongside him and Terry McDermott was a dream come true. I hadn't been good enough earlier in my career, but when I got the chance to come back that September it was unbelievable. I never thought it would happen. When we arrived, my wife Sandra and I lived in the County Hotel opposite the Central Station for about six months, and it was just fantastic to be home. I'm lucky to be from here! Places like the Tyne Bridge and the High Level Bridge make me feel very proud. I wouldn't swap this city for the world. To play in the team, my team, was great. Everyone was just so nice!

I'd been a fan when I was young, though I couldn't afford to go to the games. I was determined to get on that field and play... but I never thought it would really happen. We got promotion in my first season, and were back into the big time. That season had some great games and brilliant goals. I remember beating Manchester City 5-0, when I scored a hat trick. That's something that will live with me forever. We had beaten Cardiff, away, on the Tuesday night (19 October 1983) when I scored my first goal for Newcastle, then to score three goals in my first home game on the Saturday was amazing. We beat Brighton in the last game of that first season.

Kevin was and is such a special man and in that one year he treated me like a son, one of his own; he protected me and looked after me. I was only 22. I had been out in Vancouver for the three summers before that, and to come back to my own home town was very good, especially at a time when we were winning games, and the fans were excited and happy. There was only a 36,000 capacity at St James Park but every week it was full.

The last game in 1984 when Kevin left was quite funny. He still had his kit on at the time and when he was about to get into the helicopter he took his shirt off. I thought, that was funny, but I saw him give it to a policeman. Kevin flew from the ground to the Gosforth Park Hotel while the rest of us went in cars, with our families, for a big do up there. When we arrived, Kevin asked me, did you get my shirt? He'd given it to the policeman but he'd told him to give it to me … of course we never saw it again. I bet that policeman's not a policeman any more!

There were no low points at all, living in Newcastle in the 1980s. The club was on an up, there were people like Gazza coming through and Chris Waddle, and the three of us played very well together.

When I flew back to Newcastle after playing in the World Cup in 1986 there was a lovely crowd just to meet the plane. We'd been beaten, but that didn't matter. That day made me realise what being a footballer for Newcastle meant. They were all waving and saying well done. They really take you to their heart. It's easy to say nice things, but the people here mean it. I'm lucky now that my children grew up here and it's gone full circle.

When we weren't playing, we used to go to the Casa Italia in Low Fell, and the Godfather on Market Street. We used to eat a lot in town at Mark Toney's. In those days nobody bothered me, they were really nice, really respectful. We'd go out as a team onto the Quayside, to Julies and the other clubs, not when we were playing of course! We'd go into town and play snooker at the White Spot in China Town. The Co-op, the Odeon. I love the city. I've signed a lot of autographs!

I remember training at Hunters Moor, which was where the club trained in the 80s. The pitches were immaculate. We'd always go to the Oven Door café in Fenham, on Nuns Moor Road after training, me and Gazza and Chris Waddle. The club used to pay for Gazza to have his food as they were trying to make sure he ate well. We'd go every day and we'd go on a Friday before we played away. I loved going on the bus to away games – even now I'd rather go on the bus, as the atmosphere was brilliant.

In 1987 when I moved to Liverpool, I was sad in one way. I was disappointed to leave but lucky that I was going to Liverpool, which is very like Newcastle. When we won the league in my first season it made it a lot easier. When I came back six years later, it was fantastic. I wouldn't swap a day.

I never saw any hooliganism in my time. Newcastle was a happy place. People wanted us to win but we had an incredible set of away fans. They never moaned when we lost. There was that time we lost 8-1 to West Ham and I went in goal for the last part of the game and let three in. I was good in goal, but not very good in the outfield. The reaction of the fans was amazing! This was on the Monday night. The Saturday before that we had beaten Chelsea at Stamford Bridge when I scored two goals.

Peter Beardsley

Special K

I was there for Kevin Keegan's first match for Newcastle, against Queens Park Rangers. It was the first game I'd ever gone to without my dad and my brother. My dad had stopped going by then and my brother was on holiday in the south of France. He was horrified that he was going to miss the match! He tried to fly back but couldn't get a flight. So I went with two neighbours. We got there about 1pm though kick off wasn't until 3pm, and the queues were enormous. You could just pay on the day and get in. I was only 16 so couldn't have afforded a lot. It didn't cost that much. The ground was closed by 1.30, it was full!

We went into one of the side paddocks, where I had been used to going as a kid. We got by one of the

NUFC programme lent by Margaret Taylor

Chris Waddle, Kevin Keegan, Terry McDermott and the team praise the Newcastle fans 6 May, 1984. (NCJ / Mirrorpix)

barriers and stood in front of it, as if you were in front of a barrier and people pushed from behind, you didn't get crushed. When Kevin came out the noise was unbelievable. He said that when he scored it was as if the crowd sucked the ball into the net, the roar was so great. Everybody just went mad, chanting. I had been to the match quite a few times but there were never crowds like that. One of the lads I was with, a neighbour's grandson, was from Liverpool and he remembered Keegan from there, said had never seen anything like it, even in the Kop at Liverpool. It was a major signing. They only paid about £100,000 for him, which wasn't loads of money. It was just the calibre of him as a player. Up until then we were more of a club that sold big players rather than bought them.

I went to the final match too, when Keegan went off in a helicopter at the end. He would do that. He was a showman.

There was rioting during a couple of games after Keegan came, and management decided to put fences up. I more or less stopped going to matches then as the fences gave you a distorted view of the game. I never saw any trouble, but if you looked for it, it was there, and usually caused by kids.

Apart from the fences, I was put off by the condition of the grounds. In the old Milburn stand, the concrete was crumbling. You wouldn't go to the ladies' loos. And when I started working on Saturdays I just didn't have the time.

NUFC ticket lent by John Kelly

Margaret Taylor

When Keegan arrived it was the biggest thing the North East had seen for many a generation. We got an England player! It was a great incentive for regeneration. The club could get in a crowd of 32,000. I was there for Keegan's first match against QPR. And they were chanting KEEGAN! There was such warmth.

Do I recall any special match? Any game against Sunderland that we won!! Favourite matches? … probably Keegan's first and last games. But there were many more classics … maybe my favourite memory is when we played Southampton who had some great players, my son was five and it was his first match, 28 March 1987.

When Kevin Keegan went in 1984 it was the right time for him to go, you can't go on too long, you have to move on. We stayed in the First Division for a while then got relegated again. It goes back to the directorship. The old guard wouldn't buy new players. Mean! The 1980s were phenomenal, because after we had lost the glow right at the beginning, it went up again. We live in the world of make believe because we never got into the cup final! It's a religion up here.

John Allan (Football John)

What a blessing!

We had won promotion to the First Division and we were wondering how to celebrate. One of the lads suggested that we should go to the game in fancy dress. We agreed that would be great but who suggested that we go dressed as holy men I still do not know.

On the day of the game we met in town, a priest, a pope, a monk and a wild west padre, and made our way to Rosie's Bar on the corner of Stowell Street. On our way there we kept being stopped by people wanting to take our photos. By the time we got to Rosie's the place was heaving, so after a couple of drinks we made our way up to the ground for the game.

Almost as soon as we took our seats a policeman beckoned the four of us over to him. Our first thoughts were that we were going to be thrown out, but before we could protest he said that his 'Super' had seen us enter the ground and would we like to walk around the perimeter just to add a bit more fun to the day? We did not have to be asked twice and we were soon on the pitch, waving and having a laugh with over 40,000 Geordies. The noise was terrific. I spotted my father, my wife and son frantically waving at us from the crowd. Dad had a smile on his face as wide as the Tyne!

As we passed the tunnel, the players began to come out and the roar was

Jimmy Usher

deafening. We walked towards the Gallowgate End and were at the corner flag when Kevin Keegan came over to us and asked what we were doing. We replied that as we had won promotion and this was the last game of the season we had decided to go in fancy dress for a laugh. Keegan said 'Well in that case you had better bless me for the game'. As we blessed Keegan I looked around and noticed some of the players were laughing; none more so than Terry McDermott.

We took our seats hardly believing what had just happened to us. We had been on the pitch!!

We won the game 3-1 with goals from Beardsley, Keegan (who else?) and Waddle. On our way back to Rosie's Bar we were stopped even more often for photos. and when we went in there was a cheer. We had a couple of drinks and then moved on to another pub. As we passed a telephone box one of us was dragged in by a lad on the phone. He covered the mouthpiece and said: 'Here mate wor lass iz kicking off will yi tell a that aa'm not drunk but aa'm ganna be a bit late gittin in the neet'. He uncovered the mouthpiece and said 'Here love aa'm puttin' a priest on the phone and yi knaa they divint lie!'

Wherever we went that night we were greeted with cheers, laughs and smiling faces. I went home still on cloud nine and on Sunday morning I went down to the paper shop and bought every Sunday newspaper you could think of but we were not in one of them! It was only on the Tuesday that I received a phone call from Davy from Eastbourne telling me that we *were* in a national paper. We were lucky enough to contact the photographer, Allan Glenwright, who kindly sent us some copies of what for us had been one of the best and most memorable days we could have had.

Jimmy Usher

In pursuit of justice

In 1980 I became a village bobby in Northumberland and Newcastle became a place I went to work overtime during major events, when additional police officers were drafted in. Working in the city centre sometimes came in the shape of football matches.

Thousands of loyal black and white supporters still trekked to the ground, willing their team to better things. They bought programmes and joined turnstile queues that snaked without precision around the ground, turnstiles clicking noisily as people inched their way through the narrow portals.

The Gallowgate End of St James Park was merely a huge grey concrete hill. The wall containing the turnstiles formed the outer perimeter and, once breached, led to steps that zigzagged to the crest. Once over the summit it turned into a vast grey terrace where standing supporters faced the lush green pitch.

Thick metal barriers were scattered across the terrace, which eased the movement of the crowd. Nevertheless, a regular part of the entertainment was the motion of human waves as people at the back pushed and manipulated fellow spectators. Most were left with little choice other than to flow with the weight of the crowd, which involuntarily changed their position on the terrace.

St James Park, October 1982.

A huge set of wooden gates stood on the east corner of the Gallowgate end, guarded on the inside by a steward. A knock on a small door set in the solid gate at the back of St James Park secured entry into the ground for uniformed officers and stewards. Ironically the door cut in the titanic gate was not large enough to enter without stooping while also negotiating a high step. Once the hatch was surmounted you were inside the ground's sacred perimeter. A single storey brick-built building, whose original purpose I could not guess, stood close to the gate and was at that time used as the police office. It was not designed to take the number of people who crammed into it at peak times.

Match days for police officers and spectators alike were not a place for the claustrophobic.

The first phase of the police operation was to see supporters arriving at the ground. An officer positioned outside the turnstiles was there on time to see the supporters trickle into the ground and this turned into an avalanche as the three o'clock kick-off approached. You could feel the electricity in the air as queues grew. Before the match, crowds of supporters clad in black and white stood with their pint glasses in hand outside the Strawberry pub, timing their entry to the ground to perfection.

Standing inside the ground brought its own challenges. The turnstiles were narrow but low enough for the more athletic to vault to avoid paying the entrance fee. People regularly did just that. Often when they were caught inside they were indignant and of the opinion that, as they had cleared the hurdle, they had justly qualified for entry.

Away supporters were met at Manors Railway Station, marshalled together, surrounded and then herded like cattle to the ground. Afforded no opportunity to avail themselves of the city's facilities, they were taken straight to the ground to queue at the turnstiles. No one was allowed to escape the horde. Newcastle supporters gratefully accepted the gift of an organised procession of away colours and many had chosen spots where they waited to regale their opponents with imaginative chants. It was not difficult to spot in the lyrics of their songs an unsporting pattern. They were not, as a matter of course, wishing each other the best of fortune.

The second phase was when the game kicked off and all spectators were in the ground. It was not then an offence to be in the ground under the influence of alcohol and people often appeared so drunk that they could not follow the game. It was easy to tell those who had spent all their time before kick-off in the pub. As heads followed the ball being kicked on the pitch, the inebriated struggled to keep up. At the end of the game the away supporters were not allowed to leave the ground until the home supporters were gone. Once on their own they were rounded up and marched back to Manors Station to be immediately put back on the train. Welcome to Newcastle – feel free not to come again.

Graham Pears

The Magpie Group

In 1980 we formed the Newcastle Supporters Association. We bought Crawford's old printing works in Gallowgate and 'persuaded' Vaux Breweries to convert it into 'The Gallowgate Club' HQ of the NSA. The No. 9 Bar was opened by 'Wor Jackie' – Jackie Milburn on 9 June 1980 and we had our own newspaper, *The Supporter*. Paid for by the adverts, we printed 20,000 of each edition and gave them away free at matches.

The football club wasn't progressing on the pitch. They were in the Second Division. The fans weren't happy and wanted change. We even tried to get Brian Clough as Managing Director and we very nearly succeeded! Money was tight and the board resisted all attempts to persuade them to

Kevin Keegan, Malcolm Dix (centre), and the notorious 1980s personality Robert Maxwell, May 1984.

issue new shares. We even started a 'Buy a Player Fund', and one of our targets was Kevin Keegan. At least we 'sowed the seeds' as the Club, in conjunction with Newcastle Breweries, signed him in August 1982. What we needed was someone with the financial clout to make a difference!

I had met John Hall on a number of occasions and we had a rapport when it came to doing something about Newcastle United. The club had started to sell off their playing assets (the family silver!) – Peter Beardsley, Chris Waddle and then Paul Gascoigne. Sir John and I met to discuss tactics. It was soon apparent that the NSA could guide him to the shares while he could provide the finance. He had a memorable 'session' with Bob Cass, the *Mail on Sunday* football reporter. Bob put together a great article that stripped bare the failings of the board. 'The Rescue Act' was started.

Over 18 months, from June 1988, we amassed enough shares to enable Sir John to become director. Even then it wasn't plain sailing, it took another year to achieve control and he became Chairman.

Malcolm Dix, Hon. Vice President for the life of Newcastle United Football Club

The Great North Run

The eighties may have bestowed many blessings upon sport but surely none can compare to the creation of the Great North Run. Brought to our shores by a true son of Newcastle, Brendan Foster, it's a silver thread running through our history, stretching across three decades and more. A human chain of participants … fun runners, charity raisers, health freaks, showbiz and sports celebs, wheelchair whizzers, and the very élite of athletes who run for the record books.

It was born within a fertile mind as 1980 dawned and Big Bren, having run in, and immensely enjoyed, the Auckland Marathon, as part of his preparation for that summer's Olympics in Moscow, declared: 'I'm going to do this back home in Gateshead!'

It was organised within seven months and was to be a half marathon, to finish on the Shields sea front and take in the iconic setting of the Tyne Bridge. On Sunday, 28 June 1981 a dream came true. The first GNR snaked its way across the Tyne Bridge and down a great river to the coast. Twelve thousand five hundred entries had been accepted with local heroes Mike McLeod, Jim Alder, Steve Cram and of course Foster himself at the sharp end. Oh and a little fella called Kevin Keegan, who was within a blink of an eye to weave his particular magic in St James Park where Bren was a big fan of course. KK produced the nicest of touches running in a shirt with black and white stripes down one side of it and red and white down the other. For the record, McLeod was the first winner of the GNR, a feat he repeated the following year as well. Mike was indeed King of the Road. Keegan managed to finish but his feet were so badly blistered that he had to be carried to the medical tent.

The race has simply got bigger and better as the years have rolled on. Everyone's a winner on GNR day, which is as much about those partaking in a weird assortment of outfits from funky chickens to bunny girls. Millions have been raised for an assortment of charities and all because one man left Tyneside to go to the other side of the world and returned with a dream in his hand luggage.

John Gibson

My first attempt at the Great North Run ended up with me in a wheelchair at the old Ingham Infirmary – so I did, at least, get to South Shields. But when I came round, with a topsy turvy view of the world because I didn't have the strength to raise my head from my shoulder, I didn't know I was in a hospital. I didn't know why I and dozens of others around me were in running kit. I couldn't even remember my own name. But this, appropriately perhaps, is to get ahead of myself.

I came to Newcastle in 1982 to work as a reporter on *The Journal*. The editor, Philip Crawley, was a keen runner – or jogger as they were termed back then – and had put the paper's weight behind Brendan Foster's fledgling half-marathon. The second run had just taken place and there was a buzz about it. Some of my colleagues boasted about their times, others about their blisters. The charity fundraising wasn't quite to the fore then, as it is now. I decided I must have a go – and so began my 1980s love/hate relationship with the now famous run from Newcastle to South Shields.

The Great North Runners set off down the Central Motorway, 17 June, 1984.

I'd always run a bit, school cross country and to shake off the odd hangover. So I entered the 1983 Great North Run in a mood of excitement and confidence. I did some training, including the odd 10-miler. I never ran 13 miles because I thought once past the 10-mile landmark euphoria would propel me to the t-shirts and medals. Naivety, it's probably fair to say, was rife back then, certainly on my part; and the culture of running – of mass participation generally – not quite so ingrained.

The Great North Run used to be held at the height of summer. On June 19, 1983 the sun blazed down at the start as 19,339 runners limbered up on the Central Motorway. One of them was me, clad in a pair of thin-soled gym shoes that I now realise were wholly unsuitable. I knew no better. Nor did I know that the sensible Great North Runner resists the urge to run once the gun goes off. Carlos Lopez, the eventual race winner, can be excluded from this rule, along with other élite runners with an open road before them.

For me, getting past the person in front proved irresistible – and, since I started well down the field, fatal to my dreams of GNR glory. Inadequately shod and under-trained, I came to the first water stop at the turn into Felling. If memory serves me right, there was a big barrel and plastic cups to be dipped. The water level was low, to linger was to be swallowed in the following mob … and so I gave it a miss. By the 10-mile mark I was in trouble. The sun was beating down, the shade non-existent and my legs were leaden. I remember reaching 11 miles and starting to weave. I remember nothing more.

At some later point I came round in that wheelchair, soon to be transferred to a bed and attached to a drip. There were others in similar condition around me. There was a degree of delirium; a large man kept getting out of bed and had to be restrained. A doctor kept asking pointed questions: 'What is your name?' Gradually my mental powers flickered back into life. I guiltily remembered the two friends, up for the weekend, whom I'd told: 'Wait for me at the finish. I'll be a couple of hours.'

Next day *The Journal*'s front page proclaimed 'The Great North Sun Run'. It reported how a 'medical army' had aided 2,000 heat victims. One poor man died. Myself and 50 or 60 others literally ran until we dropped, the sensible and instinctive part of the brain overriding ambition, obstinacy and stupidity to bring the shutters down before dehydration and heat exhaustion ended not just our run but everything else too.

I vowed I'd never do the Great North Run again. But I must have entered the following year because, at the last minute, on 17 June 1984, I lined up with the other 24,182 entrants and answered the DJ's amplified cry of 'Oggy, oggy, oggy', pinched from Welsh comedian Max Boyce. I had new shoes – tennis shoes, admittedly, but with proper soles – and I reconnoitred the course. I took advice. I swallowed an over-the-counter diarrhoea cure – recommended to supplement essential body salts – before the race and

I drank at every refreshment stop. I hardly broke out of a crawl before six miles and I found, to my astonishment, that I sped up towards the finish. I got a respectable time and a medal and a t-shirt which I still treasure.

I ran the Great North Run four more times, once after that photograph was taken in Pudding Chare, outside the *Journal* and *Chronicle* offices. We are smiling but

8 June 1986. David Whetstone, centre, with fellow energetic journalists Alison Street, Alistair McCall, Steve Forshaw, Jacqui Marson, Jan Frazer and Glynn Middleton.

sadness lay behind the smiles. In the 1986 Great North Run myself and other *Journal* reporters ran to raise money to establish a journalism prize in memory of our colleague Jeremy Bennington. Jeremy was a lovely fellow and The *Journal*'s medical correspondent. He was clever, sharp and funny. He was also a real adventurer. Not for him the jog to South Shields. He decided to go ice climbing in the Scottish Highlands. Roped together with a friend, they both fell and were killed. *The Journal* lost a great reporter, we all lost a friend. We had been guests at his wedding just months previously. So we smiled for the camera, we ran for Jeremy and we raised enough money for our own good cause.

Since then many admirable people have done likewise. My last Great North Run was in 1989. Nowadays I do the sponsoring and let others pound the Tarmac.

David Whetstone

John Coatsworth

Tall Ships

In July 1986 crowds gathered on the Quayside to see the Tall Ships. The Queen paid a visit and the much heralded Maritime Festival was the highlight of a fairly good year for the city. Rates were down, sports centres were opening, new shops were moving in, and there were new jobs at Walker Technology Park.

ALL HANDS ON DECK
CUTTY SARK FOR THE
Tall ships racE
15TH – 19TH JULY
AND

Newcastle
MARITIME FESTIVAL
7TH – 27TH JULY
1986

STAND AND DELIVER

Adam and the Ants, 1981

Serious stuff

I was first elected councillor for Elswick in 1980. Broadly speaking, in terms of City party politics, the 1980s rang the death knell for the Tories in Newcastle. Labour had had a very small majority in the City Council, only about six at one point, but by the end of the decade the Tories were on the way out. At local government level, Labour Party members were preoccupied with what Labour was all about, and what municipal socialism now meant. We had an uproarious time in the City Council. I was on my own for a while but eventually there were six or seven left wing rebel councillors.

Protesters make their feelings known as they turn from Newgate Street into Blackett Street, March 1981.

Arguments revolved around the recurrent budget cuts of around £3 million, £4 million and £5 million. You could reduce that by either increasing the rates, which Council Leader Jeremy Beecham was skilled in doing, dipping into the Council reserves, or shifting the Council's priorities to lessen cuts to social services, libraries and schools. We were also trying to oppose central government.

The Council had become very non-political and so we had, for example, the annual Lord Mayor-making ceremony which must have cost a fortune. Where was the socialist priority in that?.

There are some campaigns I'm quite proud of. There was a scandal over how homeless people were often put into so called 'hotels' run by gangsters but we couldn't get any agreement from the Housing

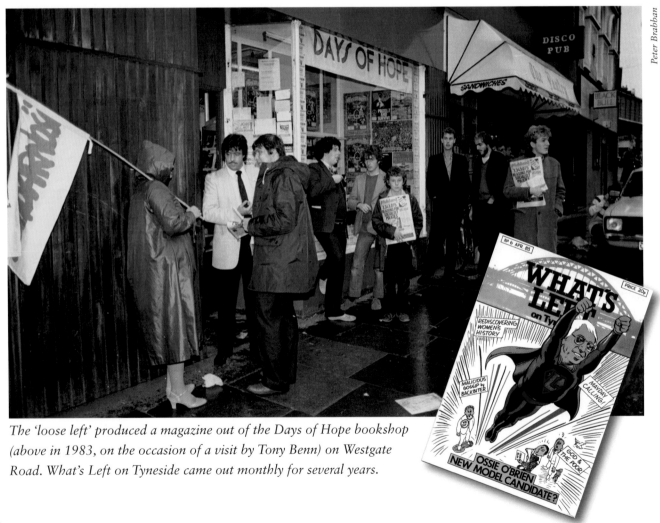

Peter Brabban

The 'loose left' produced a magazine out of the Days of Hope bookshop (above in 1983, on the occasion of a visit by Tony Benn) on Westgate Road. What's Left on Tyneside came out monthly for several years.

Committee to use their powers to intervene so I took part in a TV programme broadcast in May 1986. They exposed the national scandal and people lodged in the 'hotels' got access to proper services and had their benefits sorted out. We also abolished corporal punishment in city schools in 1981. That was very controversial and was passed on free votes that cut across Party divides. It wasn't popular with the NUT but it was a civilising step forward.

I got involved in the Campaign for Nuclear Disarmament and opposition to Cruise Missiles (I had a bit of the Greenham Common fence I waved in Council meetings!). Our aim was to persuade Councils to declare themselves Nuclear Free Zones. Quite a lot of Labour Councils did so, raising public awareness of the catastrophic consequences of nuclear war and the arms race.

Peter Brabban

Grainger Street, 1983. The suits worn by the protesters were no defence, even against paint stripper, never mind nuclear attack!

251

We tried to make it difficult for 'war games' exercises to take place, and exposed the ridiculous advice outlined in the Government's 'Protect and Survive' pamphlet of 1980. Jeremy Beecham wouldn't have us declared a Nuclear Free Zone, but he agreed to have a Nuclear Issues Working Group set up. There were two Newcastle nuclear war command centres that we knew of, plus an emergency control room under the Civic Centre. One of our victories in 1981 was to visit the two centres. One was a Civil Defence training centre hut at Sackville Terrace in Heaton, a wooden hut which the Council Officer opened up with difficulty as nobody had been in it for years. He remarked 'Do you notice anything special about this hut?' 'It's made of wood, so it's not going to withstand a nuclear attack?' He admitted that, but pointed out that it was on rails so if the earth moved after the Bomb dropped the hut would remain stable as it could move on its tracks! Then we went to see the real centre, a former RAF bunker in Blakelaw shopping centre, at the time used by Sea Cadets for training. It wasn't set up for anything much, there was a table with maps, but the Sea Cadet officers had built a well-stocked bar at the bottom of the bunker! It was very twee, and rather damp. The Nuclear Issues Group also produced a schools teaching pack, which may have been the only one of its kind in the country.

The all-consuming issue in 1984 was the Miners' Strike. Arthur Scargill was associated with the radical left and there hadn't been a proper ballot among the miners, so Jeremy Beecham wouldn't support them. Newcastle stood out as the only Labour Council in the North East that wasn't offering help to miners' families. It was such a scandal that in villages

Supporters rally in Leazes Park, 14 June 1984. Mick McGahey spoke.

From The Northumbrian Miner, August 1984.

where Newcastle bordered North Tyneside Council, one side of a street might receive food for miners' children from North Tyneside and on the Newcastle side of the street there was no help at all. Soon North Tyneside just helped everyone, to their great credit. Newcastle eventually met its statutory responsibilities but didn't go out of its way to support the miners. Out on the streets, many of us did though, and every Saturday we'd hold a public meeting at the Monument, organised by Newcastle Trades Council. There was a big march in Newcastle in 1984, and several of us went out to the Monkwearmouth picket line quite often. I was working for the Co-op which had baskets in its stores so that food could be donated.

The 1980s saw the rise of the National Front who had an office in Newcastle, in Buckingham Street, (ironically now the Sikh Gudwara) with a full-time organiser and were a sinister presence. In 1982 or 1983 the British National Party and the NF decided to hold a national march in Newcastle. A big counter demonstration was organised and the BNP march was fairly small, but it heralded the start of a period that was very threatening to black and Asian people, and to people on the left. It also saw the beginning of the Tyne and Wear Anti-Fascist Association. TWAFA became the organising core for dealing with the NF, backed and funded by Tyne & Wear Councils and is the longest running regional anti-fascist organisation in the country. Ironically, Ahmed Kutub was elected by the overwhelmingly white Fenham Ward and became a Labour Councillor in 1986, the first City Councillor from an Asian background.

Council Leader Jeremy Beecham lays the foundation stone for Elswick Road Mosque, 1985.

The presence of the NF was quite nasty and they did get some horrendous verbal support among the football crowds at St James Park. TWAFA pioneered leafleting of the ground to counteract the NF newspaper sellers outside, despite NUFC threatening to prosecute us.

They didn't appear to mind the NF sellers; they saw us as the problem! Some NF supporters were pretty unpleasant. Our tactic was to surround the NF sellers, so people had to go out of their way to buy a paper. There began to be a reaction against the racism among the fans and the club changed its attitude. Show Racism the Red Card was to grow out of this background in the 1990s.

In 1985 we chased the NF out of the Mitre pub, later the venue for *Byker Grove*. The national NF organiser, John Tyndall, disappeared out of the back window! I had a long spate of threats and abusive phone calls, and had to have police security equipment installed at home for a while. The NF stood in one or two local elections but didn't get many votes. They were a bunch of drunken thugs really.

I stood for parliament, for Central Newcastle, in the 1983 General Election. The National Union of Public Employees helped organise our campaign and we held a wonderful event, Socialism is Fun Day, which began on the Cowgate Estate. NUPE provided a trailer and people came and decorated it. The Red Umbrella band provided music and we went round the constituency holding street parties. Ossie O'Brien had been elected at a by-election in Darlington, which appeared to indicate that we would do well, but, like me, he was defeated in the General Election. It was a very lively day!

Nigel Todd

Peter Brabban

Nigel Todd, far left, on the campaign trail with Labour MP Denis Healey, Northumberland Street, May 1983.

Socialism is Fun Day, campaign lorry and passengers.
Right, Nigel and Ossie O'Brien get into the swing.

Nigel's daughter, Selina, age nine, described Socialism is
Fun Day, May 1983, for her teacher at Todd's Nook
School:

'We had a week off school and on Monday me and my friends Aimy
Kate and Anna went to the NUPE office. Anna arrived with her parents first then I
arrived with mine. Then Kate and Aimy arrived with their dad. NUPE had hired a beer lorry
and that had arrived. Christopher Maines came with his mam and so had the red umbrella band. We
helped decorate the lorry with balloons and vote labour posters and colour paper. Then some people put a bench
that belonged to NUPE and some chairs on the lorry. We sat on the bench and red umbrella sat on the chairs and
played tunes. We stopped at places and gave out stickers. Lauras mam painted faces.'

The general feeling was, video game enthusiasts aside, that Nuclear War was a bad thing, and many of the local councils had new signs erected declaring themselves to be 'Nuclear Free Zones' – presumably concluding that these would prevent radiation from passing through their boundaries, or cause missiles that could read English to glide on by, hopefully to explode over somewhere else. Preferably run by the Tories.

Several of my student colleagues had discovered protesting – with the Anti Nazi League and Rock against Racism probably being the most popular organisers, depending on whether fighting, or fighting with a musical accompaniment was your preferred sport. However, if you were a girl, your destination was probably the Womens' Peace Camp at Greenham Common, which several of my lady friends had visited and discovered short hair and dungarees.

In the early 1980s, everywhere else seemed to be having riots. Brixton, Toxteth, Handsworth, Tottenham. At first, you got the feeling that because the potential rioters of Newcastle hadn't had the first one, they weren't going to bother, so it was another ten years before we properly got in on the act (with spectacular results in North Tyneside and Scotswood). I recall somebody did set fire to a fur shop in Northumberland Street, but not because they wanted to steal the contents. It turned out to be animal rights activists.

Roland Finch

Do they know it's Christmas?

On Tuesday 23 October 1984 the 1980s reached a watershed moment when the prevailing 'me culture' promoted by Margaret Thatcher's government clashed head on with human compassion and compassion won. That was the day when Michael Buerk's film from the famine areas of northern Ethiopia was broadcast. I had been working at Oxfam for about year and was aware from Oxfam sit-reps of the growing crisis, I was also aware that Oxfam and the other agencies had been lobbying our Government and the EEC to increase aid to the area. The appeal fell on deaf ears.

As the week rolled on those of us in the Oxfam regional office became aware that something extraordinary was happening as shop after shop reported that donations to help with the crisis were flooding in. We decided to send our very own relief shipment to Ethiopia, a flight that we named 'The People's Plane'. Over the weekend the great and the good of the North East community were contacted to support our appeal and on the Monday morning a press conference was held to launch it.

Supporting the campaign were broadcaster Mike Neville (despite having a broken leg), Lindisfarne, David Jenkins (then Bishop of Durham) and others. The response exceeded our expectations, more than covering the cost of the flight, which left Newcastle Airport the following Friday.

We decided to continue the fundraising for another, bigger, regionally funded relief shipment 'The People's Boat', which left Tyne Dock just after Christmas 1984.

Peter Brabban records a TV interview about the People's Plane.

The total amount raised for the Oxfam North East appeals for Ethiopia (the People's Plane and the People's Boat) was £4.65 million. £2 million of this was raised from individuals, the rest was funds negotiated from the EEC, the UK Government and local authorities. Oxfam analysis of donations made for Ethiopia showed that the poorer parts of the UK were, by far, more generous than the wealthier regions and, in terms of the percentage of income donated, the North East was the most generous of all.

We were receiving a stream of enquiries from people wanting to do more than donate, people who wanted to know why the disaster had happened, why disasters like Ethiopia kept happening and what could be done about it. From these enquiries the 'Hungry for Change' movement sprang up. Groups of individuals, as well as organisations invited Oxfam to speak to them about the crisis. Travelling the region night after night I talked about the links between poverty and hunger, how our own policies and practices in aid, trade and debt repayments locked countries in the developing world into a cycle of poverty and how it was always the poor who paid the price when poverty spilled over into disaster.

From these meetings a network of Hungry for Change groups sprang up taking the message to the streets and shopping centres, talking to people, distributing literature and taking donations. The first major action of the movement in the North East was called Move the Mountain and took place outside the Baltic Flour Mill on 30 November 1984, the day after the Band Aid single *Do they Know it's*

Christmas was released. The Baltic was an EEC Intervention Store containing thousands of tonnes of surplus grain generated by the Common Agricultural Policy. Hundreds of Hungry for Changers and others gathered outside the Baltic to request that the grain being stored on our behalf, about 20 kilos per person, be released so that it could be sent to Ethiopia. No grain was released that night, but the publicity created by the demonstration provoked a debate that eventually led to the EEC shipping thousands of tonnes of grain to the famine areas. Central to that debate were the North East MEPs who attended the demonstration.

Hungry for Change carried on long after the Ethiopia crisis subsided, raising awareness about poverty in the developing world, lobbying MPs and MEPs about the central issues of aid, trade and debt and calling attention to the plight of poor people in places like Southern Africa, Nicaragua and Cambodia. The work of these committed and compassionate activists for the poor, took a long time to come to fruition. But it is thanks to the Hungry for Changers, and others, that the British Government eventually adopted the UN target of 0.8% of GNP as aid to the developing world (this is still being challenged by right wingers today), the creation of a consumers' Fair Trade movement and, in 2008 at the Edinburgh G8 summit, the writing off of loans from the UK to the poorest of countries. I felt that the commitment shown by so many in the winter of 1985 had finally paid off.

Peter Brabban

Peter Brabban

Hungry for Change Walk for the World, Greys Monument, 1986.

258

RIDE ON TIME

Black Box, 1989

The Metro opens!

When I started working for the Passenger Transport Executive, I came straight from school into the accounts department to deal with money relating to the building of the Metro. I wasn't quite the tea boy but was not far removed. The office, in Cuthbert House beside the Tyne Bridge, was vibrant – all the engineers were there. It was exciting for a kid straight from school. Things had to be done quickly, and it felt busy and important. I didn't get an early trip on the Metro but some of my colleagues did.

The photo shows the opening of the QE2 Metro Bridge over the Tyne on 6 November 1981. They built a little 'greenhouse' affair by the track, and the dignitaries stood in there. The staff were invited to view it. This is on the Newcastle side by Forth Banks. I'm in the crowd with lots of others.

Everything went smoothly with no major hiccups. The Queen started at Haymarket, then came by Metro to the bridge where she cut the ribbon. It looks

The Queen opens the QE2 Metro Bridge, 6 November, 1981.

pristine but we had to get there through an old dilapidated warehouse. The queen didn't get muddy! The Metro opened for passengers in August, 1980, but the official opening wasn't until the next year. The line was opened in stages. Haymarket to Tynemouth in 1980, Haymarket to Heworth in 1981, and on to South Shields in 1983.

My first trip on the Metro wasn't long after it opened as I lived near Wansbeck Road. I'd walk to Haymarket to get home. There was nothing else like it in the country. It was new and big. It felt special.

On 4 August 1981 the Byker Metro Viaduct was still under construction. It was obviously rather a hot day!

The train was a one person operation and there were no guards. You got inspectors of course. The stations had ticket machines and were unmanned.

The plan was to integrate with the buses, which would go to the main interchanges where passengers could take the Metro to the city centre. That worked until 1986 when the buses were deregulated.

Phil Richardson

Allan Finlay

Phil Richardson

When the Metro opened. I lived near Four Lane Ends so I could hop on the Metro and be in Jesmond or the centre of town in minutes. It was wonderful, so rapid, and the trains were very frequent. It was almost a door-to-door service! It seemed safe, clean and new. Four Lane Ends was an interchange so you could catch a bus to anywhere, and they were all integrated.

Kath Cassidy

Going up in the world at Haymarket, 16 September, 1982.

As the mother of three young children, the early 1980s passed in a blur of perpetual motion. The baby got half a feed before it was time to get one to school and another to playgroup, both in opposite directions and without a car. The second-hand Maclaren double-buggy was hard to steer and kept falling apart. I squeezed in the other half of the feed before it was time to collect again.

Thank goodness we lived in a city with good public transport. The first phase of the Metro opened in 1980 from the coast to Haymarket, shortly followed by the link through the city centre and out to South Shields, so we could get to the beach in either direction. The No. 33 bus also ran every few minutes into town, though I wouldn't have attempted to get a buggy on those buses, with their high steps, lack of parking space, and smoky upper decks.

Fiona Clarke

You wait for ages, then …

We had benefitted from a fairly cheap, publicly owned Tyne & Wear public transport system where the bus timetables were integrated with the Metro but this was lost after deregulation, or the start of privatisation, in 1986. The immediate effect was that overnight we got a lot of grotty bus operators. One outfit had even bought a lot of old pit buses and put them on the routes; they were really uncomfortable, and the companies were all competing with each other. It was a complete shambles.

Nigel Todd

Busways became an operator for Tyne & Wear in 1986. You might see buses from different companies overtaking each other to be first to the bus queues. You'd wait for ages, and then several would come, all in different colours, with different fares, and different routes. The unpopular routes suffered of course, and many fares rose; 5,000 bus stops had to be changed. We got used to it, and it slowly settled down.

Getting home for last orders

I travelled to London a lot in the 1980s. During 1984-5, that voyage by car was regularly extended by an hour or more courtesy of police roadblocks in South Yorkshire. Any young man from the North East travelling south was a potential flying picket, so far as the hordes of police patrolling the Miners' Strike were concerned, especially if he shared a car with a few of his mates. Of course, you could make the trip by train. Having a young person's rail card got you there half price, but it also meant no travel out of King's Cross during peak hours, which in British Rail's world was weekdays 4.30 to 7.30 pm.

You could just about get to London before the pubs closed at 11, but not the other way, because in Newcastle, last orders was still 10.30pm. Then somebody came up with the idea of toilets for buses, and all of a sudden there was a 'Blue Line' coach which promised London to Newcastle in under five hours. Non stop! The advert said the 5.30pm bus would arrive outside Legends in Grey Street around 10pm. Some chance! I think I only ever got a pint in once in about two years.

I even saved my pennies and, on a couple of occasions, booked a seat on an aeroplane. What luxury! I remember vividly it cost £33 'apex' one way, if you booked months in advance. That was a small fortune then. On those joyous occasions, my five hour bus trip home suddenly became a 50 minute flight, punctuated by a free gin and tonic.

Roland Finch

The end of the decade, summer 1989. There was another march. The NALGO strike resulted in a long overdue pay rise.

The sun was shining and there was a good view from above the Odeon's portico. Geordies were making the best of things, as usual.

The contributors